# Inside The Mountains

## A HISTORY OF MINING AROUND CENTRAL CITY, COLORADO

### BY
### TERRY COX

### FOREWORD BY
### DUANE A. SMITH

Pruett *P* Publishing Company

Boulder, Colorado

First Edition

1  2  3  4  5  6  7  8  9

Printed in the United States of America


**Library of Congress Catologing–in–Publication Data**

Cox, Terry, 1950–
    Inside the mountains: a history of mining around Central City, Colorado/by Terry Cox.
        p. cm.
    Bibliography: p.
    Includes index.
    ISBN 0–87108–761–8
    1. Gold industry—Colorado—Central City Region—History. 2. Gold mines and mining—Colorado—Central City Region—History.
    3. Mineral industries—Colorado—Central City Region—History.
    4. Mines and mineral resources—Colorado—Central City Region—History. I. Title.
HD9536.U53C63   1989
338.2'741'0978862—dc19                                      89–3555
                                                              CIP

Cover photo: Seventy years ago, owners of this 290–foot deep shaft decided mining was no longer profitable and shut the operation down. For fifteen years, they'd watched 12,000 ounces of gold and 44,000 ounces of silver move through its doors. While most structures of this vintage have crumbled, the Pozo hoist house still stands at Nevadaville.—*Author's Photo.*

# ACKNOWLEDGMENTS

Like every writer, I've depended on scores of people who've helped with gifts of time, knowledge, and perceptions. I'd like to thank all of you, but I don't even know all your names. I certainly owe my gratitude to the dedicated and especially competent librarians who came to my rescue at the Denver Public Library, the Colorado Historical Society, the University of Colorado, the Colorado School of Mines, the U.S. Geological Survey, the Bureau of Mines, and the Jefferson County Public Libraries.

I also enlisted the insights and skills of many tolerant friends. Among them were Fred Ramirez, who drafted the numerous maps you'll see, and Tom Woodruff, who drew all the illustrations. Lynda Cox, Lynn Desourdy, Max Hannum, Dennis Stevens, Joe Baird, and Kent Loest all proofread my manuscript and helped make it understandable for non-technical readers. At Pruett Publishing, Merilee Eggleston copyedited the final draft and cleaned up all the annoying mistakes I'd overlooked. To all of you, my sincere thanks.

# CONTENTS

# FOREWORD

In his classic 1867 account, *The Mines of Colorado*, Ovando Hollister stated it simply: "Gilpin is the smallest as it is the richest county of Colorado." As an experienced mining reporter and newspaperman, Hollister had seen it all over the past few years—both the boom and the bust of the Colorado mining frontier—but he never lost faith.

It was a faith well placed; Gilpin County emerged as Colorado's greatest gold district until Cripple Creek burst on the scene in the 1890s. Terry Cox takes the reader of today backwards in time to that wonderfully exciting era to capture the spirit of an age and an industry that are now gone. The reader should beware lest he or she contract a terminal case of mining fever from this enthusiastic story. The Gilpin County miners would understand this phenomenon—they were attracted by that lure and traveled down mining's trail, as did generations of Colorado miners tramping to Caribou, Leadville, Silverton, Crested Butte, and a hundred other camps and towns.

The whole saga is included in these pages, which hold a real potpourri of history, geology, individual mine stories, hints on panning for gold, and a marvelous selection of photographs, maps, and drawings. Gilpin County comes alive.

The Pikes Peak rush of 1859 grew into golden reality with John Gregory's discovery of gold between future Black Hawk and Central City. Before that time, rumor and hope substituted for gold in the pan. For the next thirty years, Gilpin County was Colorado gold country for the public, investors, miners, and smeltermen. Its towns made up the urban heart of the mountains, at least until Leadville and its silver surpassed them in the late 1870s. Its mines were some of the largest, wealthiest, most industrialized, and best equipped with modern technology that the territory, and then the state, had to offer.

In the August 30, 1862, issue of Central City's *Mining Life*, the editor wrote, "Colorado is eminently a miners' region. Its chief resources relate especially to mining of ores, and its principal interests lie directly in that branch of industry." His readers enthusiastically concurred with this assessment; there seemed to be no reason to quibble with such a truism. *Inside the Mountains* once more tells why it is true and deepens the reader's appreciation for Colorado's mining heritage.

Duane A. Smith

When you see a sign like this anywhere in Colorado, believe it.—*Author's Photo*.

# DISCLAIMER AND WARNING

This book is about the history of mining around Central City, Colorado. It is not intended to be a guidebook. The author, publisher, and distributors recognize that extreme hazards exist in and around all of the old mines in the district and expressly warn that EVERYONE STAY OUT of old mines.

Every year, several people are killed in Colorado as a direct result of old mines. There is always the clear–cut danger of falling into open shafts, but there are less obvious dangers as well. It is possible to plunge through openings plugged with last winter's snow and ice, and old ladders and wooden structures are usually rotten and decrepit; they may collapse without warning. In some mines, rotting wood gives off hazardous gases.

All old mines were worked by drilling and blasting with dynamite, so the walls and ceilings of every mine are cracked and prone to sudden collapse. The floors of many mines are partially water–filled. That mineralized water hides many hazards. At higher elevations, ice often covers the floors of mines year–round. That ice can send explorers plunging down deep shafts or into inescapable traps. Even dry gravel floors can be hazardous when the gravel covers up old, wooden, temporary floors. Temporary floors weren't safe a hundred years ago. They are extremely dangerous today.

Many mines have branching passages, and it is easy for explorers to become disoriented, scared, and lost. If they haven't told anyone where they are going, timely rescue can be impossible.

Lawful access to the mines is yet another matter, because all mines are now privately owned, and few landowners allow exploration. Trespassing is a separate hazard, often involving firearms or lawmen.

The author, publisher, and distributors expressly warn readers to stay out of old mines, and they assume no liability relative to the use of this book.

# AREA THIS BOOK COVERS

This book focuses almost entirely on the heart of the mining area around historic Central City, Black Hawk, Nevadaville, and Russell Gulch. While there has been a considerable amount of gold, silver, copper, and tungsten removed from other parts of Gilpin County, the area covered here was both the most heavily mined and the most economically important.

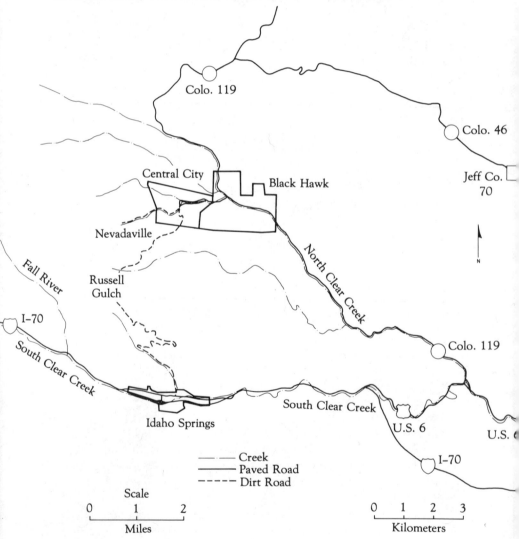

Colo. 119

Colo. 46

Central City

Black Hawk

Jeff Co. 70

Nevadaville

Fall River

Russell Gulch

North Clear Creek

I-70

South Clear Creek

Colo. 119

Idaho Springs

South Clear Creek

U.S. 6

U.S. 6

I-70

N

—————— Creek
——————— Paved Road
- - - - - Dirt Road

Scale

0    1    2
Miles

0    1    2    3
Kilometers

# INTRODUCTION

Underground mining is a dirty, dangerous, backbreaking profession. Still, mining, and especially gold mining, has always held a certain lingering mystique. There's something about gold mining that's fascinating, that captures our imaginations.

Part of that fascination is "gold fever." Gold fever battered the country hard after the 1848 discovery of gold in California. Gold fever was a communicable disease, spread by newspapers and worsened by rumors. Starvation was the only dependable cure. Its victims flocked to purported gold finds and built boomtowns overnight, but they couldn't settle down. They always knew the big bonanza was waiting just over the next mountain. So they moved on and left faded ghost towns behind as lingering reminders of the disease.

In 1858, ex–California prospectors found small gold deposits on the high plains east of the Rocky Mountains. As the news spread, a bout of gold fever followed, and it spawned the new town of Denver City. Prospectors set off for the mountains and soon found large, rich gold deposits there. When word of the new finds hit the plains, gold fever quickly spread all the way to the East Coast. The gold rush was on.

But what has happened since? Is gold fever gone? Has the modern world developed an immunity to it? Hardly.

Think back to the gold craze of 1980. Americans everywhere tore apart dressers and trunks searching for their old class rings and junk jewelry. Why? Because gold was worth $852 an ounce and they wanted to sell.

The price of gold has certainly fallen far below those dizzying heights, but radio and TV still carry daily gold quotes in their financial reports. Why? Does the ordinary person really have so much gold stashed away that day–to–day fluctuations are critical?

No. Gold fever may be in remission, but it's still here. It's still uncured.

How many restaurants have you seen decorated with mining themes? They're everywhere, even in places distant from the gold fields. Drive up to Central City and Black Hawk some summer day. How many people do you see hunkered over gold pans along Clear Creek?

Would you like to see a real–life example of what gold fever was like a hundred years ago? Walk into any prospecting store in Denver and you'll find victims still telling tall tales and swapping lies. If you're polite, they might even show you one of their nuggets. But don't expect them to tell you where they found their treasures. Secrecy is another time–honored symptom.

This book, then, is for those incurable romantics who still have a bit of the fever. For those people who walk through Central City and still quietly wonder if "there's any gold still left in these mountains?"

Panning for gold. Gold found in the sand and gravel along streams is called placer gold.—*Courtesy Western History Collection, University of Colorado.*

# EARLY COLORADO GOLD HISTORY

Gold mining helped settle the region and helped the region become a state. Ironically, though, no one knows who first discovered gold. Or where the discovery was. Early mountain men, Indians, and explorers certainly knew gold occurred in the Rocky Mountains, but few writings remain. It's not that one of them found gold and wanted to keep it secret. Rather, gold was just not that important. Certainly not as important as food, furs, and survival.

The earliest rumors of Colorado gold probably stem from small finds in the San Juan Mountains and date from the time Spain controlled the region. The first written mention of gold in the area is in Zebulon Pike's historic account of his explorations of 1806–1807. Apparently, a mountain man had found gold somewhere along the South Platte River and related the story to Pike.

The first confirmation of gold in Colorado, however, came on the heels of the great gold rush to California in 1849. Most prospectors took hurried northern and southern routes around the high mountains. A few, however, tried their luck in Front Range streams on their way west. Among them were men such as John Beck, Louis Ralston, and William Greene Russell, who made the first confirmed discoveries of gold. Their finds, however, were no match for the promise of wealth they thought awaited them in California, and they moved on.

## The Discoveries of 1858 and the Rush to Denver

Like the majority of the Forty–niners, Russell and Beck never made it big in California. Having already made tentative finds there, they decided the high plains of western Kansas (which later formed the nucleus of Colorado Territory) was their next best bet for finding gold. In the winter of 1857, Russell and Beck decided to organize a party the next spring to investigate their earlier finds.

With a party of 104 men, they set out on April 25, 1858, for the upper reaches of Cherry Creek in western Kansas. By mid–May, they reached their goal near present–day Franktown and began prospecting. Nearby, the group found meager signs of gold at the site of one of Beck's 1849 finds, but decided to move on and look for more.

Over the next three weeks, the group prospected several spots along the South Platte River and the Vasquez Fork (Clear Creek). They tried parts of Ralston Creek and even followed it five miles into the mountains. James Pierce was a member of the Russell contingent and, in an unpublished manuscript on file at the Colorado Historical Society, said they were in the mountains for "several days but found nothing of importance." He added, however, that they "got gold every pan." Even though they were finding gold, Beck was disheartened at the size of their discoveries. With most of the seventy–seven men he had brought, he headed back east on June 10.

After trying to find gold in Boulder Creek, the Big Thompson, and Bear Creek, the remaining group turned back toward the Platte. Another thirteen men gave up there, and by the end of June, Russell's remaining party consisted of thirteen diehard prospectors. They kept looking for gold and soon found better diggings on Dry Creek (a small tributary to the Platte located in present–day Englewood). The deposit was small, but they managed to dig out a few hundred dollars in gold.

While they were working the Dry Creek find, a man named Cantrell appeared. Pierce said Cantrell "had been to Fort Laramie in the Black Hills trading with the Government troops and had heard about our party starting out from Leavenworth and had concluded to come by and see what we were doing." Cantrell ended up taking a bag of dirt from their prospect back to Kansas City. There, he panned it in front of witnesses and told them Russell's party had found a thousand dollars worth of gold in ten days.

Like all news about gold, word of the discovery spread like wildfire. As usual, the stories grew with each telling. The previous year's recession, known popularly as the Panic of 1857, had financially decimated people all across the Midwest. They were ready for good news—true or not. By the end of August, newspapers as far away as Boston had parroted the tale of gold finds on the high plains. Having no established town names to use, they referred to the area as the "Pikes Peak" region. Never mind that the famous mountain was sixty miles south of the gold discoveries.

In retrospect, Russell's group probably found only thirty to forty ounces of gold during the whole summer of 1858. Even Russell was unimpressed and knew that was barely enough to get excited about. In fact, he left ten men behind and headed back to Georgia for the winter. The newspapers, however, paid little heed to the facts in their stories of gold. Midwesterners would hardly have listened anyhow.

Only the most adventurous set out for "Pikes Peak" so late in the year. By the Christmas of 1858, though, there were probably a thousand men camped along the South Platte looking for gold. By the next spring, the trickle had turned into a flood. Spurred on by misleading guidebooks and overblown rumors, people descended on the fledgling towns of Auraria and Denver City in droves. After all, they expected to find gold lying on the banks of the Platte. Gold fever became a high plains epidemic.

The reality of life on the frontier, though, cured many would–be millionaries of the fever. They discovered that it was hard to find gold and there wasn't much gold to find. Discouraged, many headed back east and tried to warn the westbound pilgrims of the folly ahead. Few believed them, though, thinking the quitters were trying to keep all the gold to themselves.

Most of the guidebooks had been outrageous in their claims of gold finds. Some were total fabrications. But most weren't completely wrong. There truly was a little gold in a few streams on the plains, and the sensible people knew they couldn't get rich working there. In his manuscript, James Pierce commented, "As yet nothing worthy of the excitement had even been found; in fact, nothing but some little deposits near the Platte and the light float gold on Cherry Creek and a little bar on Ralston and Gold on Clear Creek—these were all that had been found up to that time."

Newcomers must have reasoned that the streams had washed the gold from elsewhere, but few knew how to look for the source. The few who did were seasoned prospectors who'd worked in the California gold fields. Recognizing similarities to rich California discoveries, many suspected the best gold deposits were to be found in the mountains. One of those prospectors was George Jackson.

Apparently the first to find gold in the mountains, Jackson found a deposit near present–day Idaho Springs in January of 1859. At about the same time, other prospectors discovered gold about twelve miles farther north along two branches of Boulder Creek.

So far, prospectors had been looking for placer gold, the gold they found in streams. Because of its extreme density, miners could easily separate placer gold from the sand and gravel. Stream deposits, however, were small, and they always played out quickly.

For centuries, miners had known they could trace the placer deposits upstream. If they were patient and thorough, they could find where the placer gold had come from. Nobody had yet done that in Colorado. By this time, though, there was another Georgia miner already looking. Looking for a rich gold vein in the mountains. When he found it, he effectively emptied the towns down on the plains.

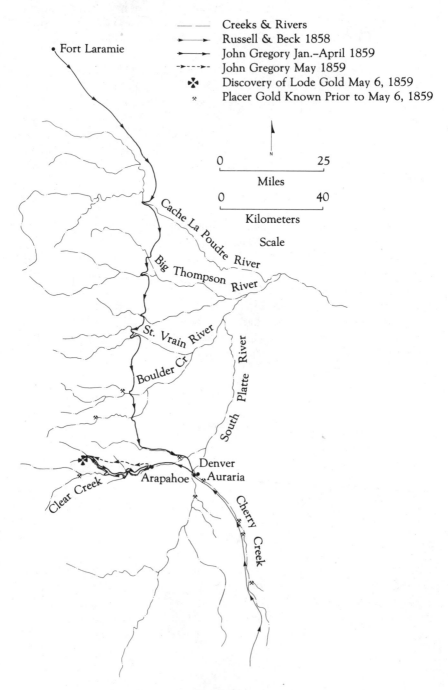

**JOHN GREGORY'S ROUTE—1859**

Creeks & Rivers
Russell & Beck 1858
John Gregory Jan.–April 1859
John Gregory May 1859
Discovery of Lode Gold May 6, 1859
Placer Gold Known Prior to May 6, 1859

Fort Laramie

Cache La Poudre River

Big Thompson River

St. Vrain River

Boulder Cr

South Platte River

Denver
Auraria
Arapahoe

Clear Creek

Cherry Creek

N

0        25
Miles

0        40
Kilometers

Scale

# HISTORY OF THE DISTRICT

## The Gold Discoveries of 1859

It was forty-year-old John H. Gregory who turned the course of Colorado history. Working in Wyoming at the time, he heard the news of gold discoveries in the Pike's Peak region and set out to find some gold for himself. It was still winter, early in 1859, but he prospected many icy streams on his southward journey. He apparently found little gold until he tested sands of Clear Creek.

Sampling the sands of Clear Creek as he worked his way into the mountains, he found enough gold to keep going. About fourteen miles above Golden, he discovered that the creek forked into two main branches (today, the junction of State Highways 6 and 119). He panned gold from both branches of the creek, but discovered that the northern fork was the richer of the two.

He continued prospecting upstream, testing each gully and waterway that joined the main creek. As he worked up the North Fork, he noticed the gold flecks in his pan becoming coarser and more plentiful.

About seven miles above the forks (where Black Hawk is now located), he tested a tributary gulch and found even more gold. Working westward into the side stream, he passed a small side gully to the south and noticed an immediate decrease in the amount of gold. Experience in California told him the source of his gold was near at hand and he'd just passed it. It was now April and it was snowing and Gregory was excited.

He started carrying dirt from the hillsides down to the small stream to pan. He wanted to pinpoint the vein, but the snow kept falling heavier and he knew he had to quit. Freezing and dangerously short of provisions, Gregory sadly retreated to the plains before he found his bonanza.

At the small town of Arapahoe, Gregory met a party of newly arrived prospectors from Indiana led by Wilkes DeFreese. Normally a loner, Gregory must have trusted DeFreese, because he shared his precious secret. Together they plotted to explore the find more thoroughly as soon as the snows melted.

Accompanied by his new friends, Gregory once again found the likely spot he'd located a few weeks before. On May 6, 1859, racing another spring storm, he panned dirt from the first lode found in the Colorado mountains and secured an untouchable niche in Colorado history.

The soil and dirt from the first lode was far richer than any placer found so far in the Pikes Peak region. It was everything Gregory could have hoped for. According to Gregory, his first pan of dirt yielded a phenomenal $4 in gold, or about a quarter of an ounce. That much gold would be worth about $87 today.

The party named the vein after Gregory and promptly staked out 100-foot-long claims. As the discoverer, Gregory retained two claims, #5 and #6. Both were located a couple of hundred feet above the bottom of the gulch. DeFreese took claim #4, and the thirteen remaining members took a claim apiece on the vein as they traced it from the gulch up the hillside.

The men knew the deposit was very rich, but another deep spring snow prevented them from working it for ten more days. By the twenty-third of May, though, the melting snows provided enough water for their pans and sluices and everyone recovered a lot of gold. Within a week, Gregory took over fifty ounces of gold from the #5 claim alone. He mined more gold in a week than Russell's party had found during the whole previous summer down

This is one of the earliest known photographs of the Gregory Diggings near Black Hawk. Based on the number of buildings, the amount of undisturbed dirt, and the number of standing trees, this shot was probably taken in either 1859 or 1860. In the distance, directly over the heads of the people tending the sluice, are the diggings on the Gregory vein.—*Courtesy Western History Department, Denver Public Library.*

Shortly thereafter, William Byers, owner of the new Denver newspaper, the *Rocky Mountain News*, visited the "Jackson Diggings" and the "Gregory Diggings" on behalf of his interested readers. To his amazement, he found all the rumors of the discovery were true. Hurriedly, he printed a special issue of the paper to tell the story. The news, this time factual, was shouted across the Midwest, and the beginnings of the gold rush were on.

Within days, hundreds of men streamed into Gregory Gulch and the surrounding countryside. They claimed everything they could find. By June, there were several thousand people in the area; and they founded many towns, including Gregory Point, Mountain City, Black Hawk, Central City, and Russell Gulch.

The rush, while mad, was fairly orderly thanks to rules drawn up by Gregory and Dr. Joseph Casto, one of the Hoosiers. Using California mining laws as their model, they formulated plans for the fair division of veins, placers, and

## How Prospectors Found The Veins

How could the old-time prospectors have found all the gold veins around Central City? Even when you see the veins in person, it still seems perplexing.

What the prospector did, though, was the essence of simplicity. He dug up gravel near a creek, washed it in a rusty steel pan, and looked for gold left in the bottom. If the gold was in tiny, minuscule pieces, he knew that the stream had ground it up and he reasoned that the stream had carried it a long distance from its source. On the other hand, if the gold was in larger flakes or nuggets, he knew the underground source was probably nearby.

Working upstream, the prospector tested gravel from every side gully and tributary stream. He always followed the branch of the stream that showed the most gold. In this manner, then, he constantly narrowed down the possibilities of where the vein deposit was.

Around Central City and Black Hawk, the veins occurred in such profusion that it would have been difficult finding the best deposit. Only John Gregory and his earliest associates ever had that dubious problem. Everyone else had to take what he could find.

In the highland areas with no permanent streams, prospecting was immeasurably harder. So hard, in fact, that prospectors didn't find some deposits for many years. In those situations, the prospector looked for yellowish or brownish rocks that appeared burned. If he found any, he hauled some of his dirt to the nearest stream and panned it there to see if he had any gold. His job became a little easier in the 1870s and 1880s after mining and smelting had stripped the hillsides bare of trees. Subsequent erosion soon exposed rock outcrops that were previously hidden by soil and undergrowth.

mill sites within the Gregory District. Only thirty-three days after gold was found, 2,000 to 3,000 miners gathered at Gregory Point to debate the mining laws. By that time (it was only June 8), there were already latecomers who felt cheated. There was heated dissension, but proponents of Gregory's rules successfully maneuvered the meeting. With a positive vote, the group officially established the Gregory Mining District, the first district in Colorado and the first of hundreds to come.

With so many men looking so desperately for gold, it's hardly surprising that they discovered practically all the major vein deposits during 1859. That's not to say they successfully worked all the deposits. They couldn't. Out of necessity, groups of men often banded together into loosely organized companies. Certainly the companies were better prepared to set about the business of mining than lone prospectors armed with only shovels and pans.

## Early Development of the District

The boom into the Gregory District, as all good booms do, caused tremendous shortages—and tremendous opportunities. The mining area was remote from the supply towns of Golden and Denver, and both of them were 600 miles from the nearest railroad. To meet the demand for food and other goods, construction on toll roads across the foothills began almost immediately. Even before decent roads could be finished, the typical boomtown service businesses—newspapers, banks, mills, saloons, hotels, and churches—sprang up, seemingly overnight. In this and every other gold rush across the West, some of the most successful people in town were the entrepreneurs who snatched at opportunity. In effect, they mined the pockets of the miners instead of sweating underground.

The gold fever of 1859 struck with an unstoppable vengeance. Prospectors found new gold veins almost daily and opened up mines as soon as they could find picks, shovels, and black powder. After only a couple of weeks, John Gregory was a revered "old-timer." He was also no fool and saw the trend of things to come.

Within a couple months of his discovery, he decided that mining was going to take too much physical work. He sold both of his original claims for $21,000 and cashed in on his renown as the discoverer of the district. (In 1859, the dollar was worth much more than it is today; $21,000 then would be worth nearly half a million dollars today.)

Obviously adept at the art of finding gold, Gregory became a consultant. He contracted with his new buyers, and other less experienced men, to prospect for them at the rate of $200 per day. During the summer, he located the Gregory Extension lode, the Gregory No. 2 vein, the Bates, and several others. Meanwhile, he built a small mill near the Gregory vein with part of his earnings. After it was operational, he turned around and promptly sold it, too, for six times his cost. (Gregory's $200 daily salary in 1859 equates to roughly $4,400 today.)

One of John Gregory's handwritten claims. It reads:

> Know all men by these presents that we, John H. Gregory and R.T. Rees, claim for mining purposes 100 feet long and 50 feet wide in the Gulch that runs between the Gregory Lead and the Fisk Lead in Gregory Diggings. Said claim is Number one being the 3d claim South from the Gregory Gulch.
>
> The above claim is laid out in accordance with the Mining Laws of this district.

Sept 9th, 1859                                           J.H. Gregory, R.T. Reese

Gregory was the man who started the hardrock mining industry that eventually led to the formation of the territory and the state of Colorado. He was indeed an important figure, and much has been written about his first historic year of 1859. But he was not the typical miner destined to stay in the mountains for the long haul, and he never left the commanding impression that his more politically inclined successors did.

For the next three years, he apparently spent three seasons a year in the mining district and wintered in Georgia. Records of his activities and travels, though, are rather tenuous. He apparently left the region after 1862 and was never heard from again.

Throughout the summer of 1859, development was frenzied as miners opened literally hundreds of placer and lode mines. As they discovered new deposits outside the narrow bounds of the original Gregory District, miners formed new districts. Most used mining laws copied or modified from the Gregory example. Some of the important new districts created during this period were the Nevada, Eureka, Lake, Central, and Russell Gulch districts.

Most mines showed substantial returns, and many expected conditions to be the same as those in California, where rich and easily worked gold veins extended to great depths. The gold seemed very easy to recover with little expense and less experience. All the miner had to do was dig or blast the vein rocks out of the ground and shovel the dirt into sluices. The action of the water running through wooden troughs simply carried away most of the sand and soil and left gold nuggets and gold flour trapped in the bottom. Conditions did not remain easy for long, though.

The deeper the miners dug, the harder the ore became. Within weeks, most miners knew they would have to crush their ore to get at the gold locked inside the rocks.

Early mills were rudimentary affairs. Their sole purpose was to crush ore to dust in order to free the gold particles. The first mills in the region were old Spanish–style arrastres. They were simple to build and were essentially stone grist mills designed to crush rocks. Within weeks, miners miraculously

D.H. Huyett made this woodcut for *Leslie's Illustrated Newspaper* in 1859. The mill along the creek was one that John Gregory sold to Conklin for six times his original investment. Behind the mill is a line of diggings on the Gregory vein, and to the right are rows of sluices working dirt from various claims.—*Courtesy Western History Department, Denver Public Library.*

shipped in heavy metal stamp mills from eastern foundries to supplement and replace the arrastres. Whereas arrastres crushed ore by dragging a heavy stone around a circular granite trough, stamp mills broke the ore with banks of dropping pistons. (You can see an arrastre in the courtyard of the Idaho Springs Public Library; you can see stamp mills at the Argo Mill in Idaho Springs and at several places in Central City.)

Regardless of construction, all mills used mercury amalgamation to help capture the very fine gold particles mixed up in the pulverized rock dust. The phenomenon is simple: gold particles stick to mercury and rock doesn't. Amalgamation had been known for centuries and was the mainstay of every successful gold operation in the world.

Millmen built their mills along the valleys to take advantage of free water power for crushing. By the end of summer, however, the streams were mostly dry. Plans were quickly made for the diversion of water from the higher mountains to the west, and a ditch company was soon formed. Construction began on a ditch to stretch from the head of Fall River into the heart of the mining district by the next summer.

Donated labor accomplished much of the project, and the $100,000 Consolidated Ditch opened to holiday fanfare on July 4, 1860. The beneficiaries soon stopped celebrating, however, when the found out how much the Consolidated Ditch Company intended to charge for water. The new Central City town government made several abortive efforts during the year to buy the ditch, but no deals were ever signed. The lack of cheap water certainly

Tunnels like this used to dot the hillsides from Black Hawk to Idaho Springs, but most have collapsed over the last century.—*Photo by Lachlan McLean. Courtesy Western History Collections, University of Colorado.*

hindered early development of the district, but there were more serious troubles looming in the gold field.

By late 1860, two major concerns became evident as the mines were dug deeper and deeper. First, a number of mines encountered ore zones that were much narrower at depth than they had been near the surface. Normally, the ore zone again became wider farther down, but digging through barren rock was very costly. The more insidious problem, however, was that the physical and chemical makeup of the ore changed with increasing depth.

## Problems with Sulfides

During the first year, most mines had been incredibly profitable while working ore deposits within ten, twenty, or thirty feet of the surface. The reason was that the ore had been exposed to air and water for thousands of

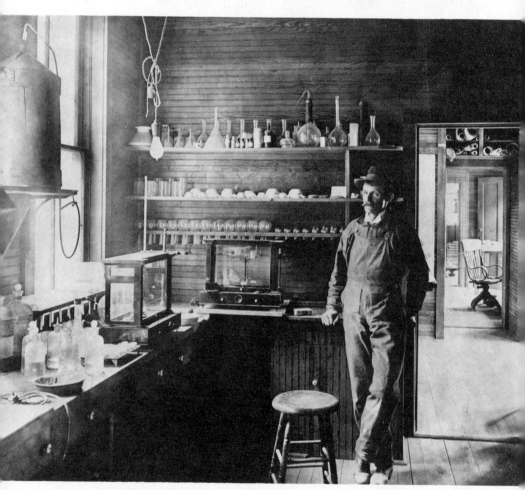

Assay laboratories like this one, owned by the Fifty Gold Mines Company, tested local ores for gold and silver content.—*Courtesy Western History Department, Denver Public Library.*

years. This slow, patient process is called weathering, and it is nature's way of milling and concentrating gold ore. Consequently, the ore near the surface yielded its treasure of gold quite easily.

With depth, however, the ore became progressively harder. It took more and more crushing to release the gold. Usually at about 50 to 150 feet below the surface, the mines hit unweathered rock, and suddenly even rich mines started losing money hand over fist. What had happened?

The men were mining the same way they always had. They were shipping as much ore as ever. It just seemed as if the gold was mysteriously gone.

The interior of the Buell mill photographed by Joseph Collier; the stamps are on the left side with the amalgamation plates below. Mercury coated the copper plates, the gold stuck to the mercury, and workers scraped the amalgam off periodically to retrieve the gold.—*Courtesy Western History Department, Denver Public Library.*

Impossible! California had never had that problem.

As it turned out, the veins were as rich as ever, but the mills just couldn't save as much gold from the deeper ores. Mines ran assays, or chemical tests, on the rock, and they showed wonderful quantities of gold in the stubborn ores. That meant the gold was still there. But the assays also showed large quantities of sulfur minerals that hadn't been present near the surface.

The assays proved that the mills were losing as much as 95 percent of the gold. For some unknown reason, the mercury no longer worked. The gold would hardly even stick to it. The miners blamed the mill operators and the millmen blamed the ore.

Slowly, but ever so surely, mines started shutting down. They just couldn't recover enough gold to stay in business. Ovando Hollister, noted mining historian of the 1860s, quoted an unnamed writer who reflected hundreds of miners' sentiments: "Somehow the mills as a general thing do not save the gold; why it is hard to tell. There must be some difficulty beyond the mills—doubtless the want of experience in the men who run them."

## GOLD FEVER

Early in the summer of 1860, I had a bad attack of gold fever. In Chicago the conditions for such a malady were all favorable. Since the panic of 1857, there had been three years of general depression, money was scarce, there was little activity in business, the outlook was discouraging, and I, like many hundreds of others, felt blue.

*A Gold Hunter's Experience*, 1898

This quote came from an interesting little book Chalkley J. Hambleton privately published for his fascinated family and friends. In his book, Hambleton told how he had owned a number of so-so claims around Nevadaville and Russell Gulch in the early 1860s. After he hit the sulphides, he couldn't get any gold for his efforts. He decided to pack it in, and he returned to the normal life he'd left in Chicago. His dreams ended, in typical understatement, with: "On the 22nd of October, 1863, I left the mountains and gave up the mining business forever."

There were hundreds of mines located on rich deposits, but the miners often could not recover enough gold to meet the costs of mining. Moreover, water seepage into the mines had become a significant problem. The miners noticed they had reached the water table at just about the same time they had reached the stubborn ores.

It was apparent to experienced miners that the sulfur minerals in the deep ores somehow prevented the gold from amalgamating with the mercury. But what could they do? They were helpless.

A forward-looking entrepreneur named Caleb Burdsall figured he might be able to smelt the ore and recover the gold that way. Smelting was an ancient process whereby operators could melt the ores in specially designed furnaces and recover the metals while they were molten. Burdsall went so far as to build a smelter in Nevadaville in 1861. Unfortunately, a disastrous fire swept through town and burned his plant to the ground before it could even be tested. Though he must have felt his idea was valid, he never rebuilt his plant.

Outside the gold fields, the region was growing by leaps and bounds. In 1861, Colorado became the nation's newest territory. Legislators divided the territory into seventeen counties, with the smallest named Gilpin and organized around Central City and Black Hawk. Although it was named in honor of William Gilpin, a famous early explorer and promoter of Colorado, heavy local sentiment favored naming it after John Gregory. The movement failed, however, leaving only the names Gregory Hill and Gregory Gulch as permanent tributes to the man who had started the gold rush two and a half years before.

By this time, factors other than the sulfide problems began to affect the financial structure of mining in Gilpin County. Back east, tensions that would lead to the Civil War had increased. Immigration into the gold fields had dropped. Prices for practically every commodity had risen to unbearable levels and were spurred higher by the first of many Indian attacks on wagon-borne supplies coming across the plains. To add insult to injury, eastern foundries started forging for the imminent war effort, and badly needed hoists, pumps, and engines became exceptionally hard to find. Was this the way gold mining in Colorado was going to end?

# Period of Consolidation

Given the difficulties plaguing the district during the 1860s, it surprised the hard-pressed miners to learn how much money eastern investors wanted to spend in Colorado. People were absolutely enthralled with the idea of investing in Colorado gold mines. It didn't matter that the field was in a decline. All that mattered was that the mines around Central City had already produced fabulous wealth and that they were for sale at excellent prices.

What followed was a two-year run on Colorado gold mining stocks. Investors hastily organized holding companies in New York, Boston, and Chicago to do business in Colorado. Through stock sales, the companies were able to buy up and consolidate large numbers of idle mines and claims. By 1863, there were over 200 Colorado mining stocks traded on the New York exchange alone.

Previously, thousands of individuals had controlled thousands of small, 100-foot-long claims. While profitable in the early days, the claims were just too small to work efficiently in underground mines. Through stock sales, however, the new holding companies could afford to buy up large blocks of claims and combine them into large, efficient mines. The consolidation made mining in the district more profitable, and Gilpin County gold production topped 84,000 ounces in 1864 to set yet another new record.

# CLAIMS

Today, a prospector may still claim a gold deposit on public property. In order to gain legal control of the land, he has to mark his discovery on the ground and file a notice with the appropriate county courthouse. He then has a valid claim. He doesn't own the land. He merely has a right to mine it.

Back in 1859, when Gregory found the first lode gold in the mountains, there were no federal claim laws. To avoid chaos, Gregory and his friends made up their own "laws" and based them on earlier California examples. They decided the sizes of the claims should be:

| | |
|---|---|
| Lode claims | 100 feet long x 50 feet wide |
| Placer claims | 100 feet long x width of stream |
| Mill sites | 250 feet long x 250 feet wide |

Other districts followed the example of the Gregory District, but changed the sizes somewhat. When Colorado became a territory in 1861, legislators gave reasonable local regulations the force of law. Finally in 1866 and 1872, the U.S. passed its first statutes for new claims on public lands. Over the years, administrators realized extremely small claims were not conducive to efficient mining and gradually enlarged the legal sizes of claims. Because of geological conditions, claim sizes still vary from state to state. In Colorado they presently are:

Lode deposits: up to 20 acres (generally 600 feet x 1500 feet)
Placer claim: up to 20 acres for an individual or
         up to 160 acres for an association of individuals

Claim laws give the locator certain rights. He has the right to mine the claim for valuable minerals. He has the right to use the surface to develop the mine. And he can sell the rights to his claim like any other piece of real estate. Ownership of the land, however, stays with the government.

Under certain conditions, an owner may patent his claim. That means he can get the government to transfer actual ownership of the surface and minerals to him. Patenting statues are now very restrictive, but were quite lax in the past. Over the years, claim holders have patented practically all their claims around Central City. So unless the land is marked otherwise, assume all land to be private.

Unfortunately, consolidation took control of the mines away from experienced local miners and put it into the hands of managers often located thousands of miles away. Management was often carried on by telegraph, but it worked only as long as the mines were able to produce easily milled ore and there were no operating emergencies.

KNOW ALL MEN BY THESE PRESENTS, That ...

... of the county of ... and Territory of Colorado; in consideration of the sum of ... Dollars to me in hand paid by ... the receipt whereof I do hereby acknowledge, have remised, released, and forever quit claimed, and by these presents do remise, release, and forever quit claim unto the said ... heirs and assigns the following described property, situate, lying and being in the county of ... Territory of Colorado, to-wit:

TO HAVE AND TO HOLD the aforesaid premises, with all the privileges and appurtenances thereunto belonging or appertaining, unto the said ... heirs and assigns, to sole use forever, so that neither the said ... heirs, nor any person or persons, claiming under ... or them, shall, at any time hereafter, by any way or means, have claim or demand any right or title to the aforesaid premises or appurtenances or to any part or parcel thereof, forever. In testimony whereof have hereunto set hand and seal this ... day of June A. D. 186 4. Signed, sealed, and delivered in presence of

TERRITORY OF COLORADO, ss.
Gilpin County.
Before me ... a Notary Public in and for the county of ... and Territory of Colorado, came ... personally known to me to be the identical person whose name is subscribed to the foregoing deed of conveyance, as having executed the same, and acknowledged the same to be his free, voluntary act and deed for the uses and purposes therein expressed.
And the said ... wife of the said ... having been by me made acquainted with the contents of said deed of conveyance, and examined separate and apart from her said husband, acknowledged that she executed the same and relinquished her right of dower in the premises mentioned, voluntarily, freely, and without compulsion of her said husband; and that he do not wish to retract the same.
In Testimony whereof, I have hereunto set my hand and affixed at my office in Central City this ... day of ... A. D. 186 ...

With this ornate piece of paper, Hannibal Kimball sold J. Fred Pierson 66 2/3 feet on the Muck lode for $1,750 in 1864. The vein must not have been profitable, because its location is now unknown.—*Courtesy American West Archives, Cedar City, Utah.*

Of course, easy capital, especially during wartime, did not last long. Nor had any solution been found for contending with the stubborn sulfides. By the end of 1864, company after company suspended business, and a new period began in the gold field: the period of the process peddler.

## Process Mania

By 1864, most mine operators, regardless of whether they lived in the East or the West, openly recognized that something had to be done to break the stranglehold of the sulfide minerals. James Lyon of Black Hawk thought the obvious answer was to resurrect Burdsall's earlier idea and build another smelter. Apparently, Lyon considered the idea as early as 1862, but he didn't do anything about it until 1865. By that time, the period of "process mania" had gripped Gilpin County and, by inference, the rest of the territory.

The typical miner was interested in his own property, not his neighbor's, and certainly not the district as a whole. Trapped by his own problems, he knew there just had to be some peculiar process that could wrest his gold from the sulfides. In desperation, he was willing to try anything. And everything. Until he ran out of money.

Recognizing the desperation, peddlers descended on the district and offered to sell all sorts of innovative processes to get the gold out of the ores. Some of the salesmen absolutely believed they were offering legitimate and viable methods for gold extraction. Others suffered no such delusions and were nothing more than traveling con artists. Many apparently aspired to higher education and boasted the unearned title of "professor" in their chosen line of work.

Ostensibly, many of the processes sounded reasonable. At least to desperate miners. Methods ranged from roasting ores with ordinary salt to treating them with secret, mysterious, and (of course) costly ingredients. Every process in the book had its proponents, who, like snake oil salesmen, claimed fantastic successes. In actual practice, none of the processes ever worked as well as promised. Still, the processes did extract gold from the district—all from company treasuries.

Hundreds of companies fall prey to the hope of finding a successsful process while the helpless stockholder paid the bills. It was the mining industry itself, however, that proved to be the ultimate victim as new investment in the state stuttered to a halt. The famous government geologist of the 1870s, Rossiter Raymond, noted "Process–mania, commencing in 1864 and lasting till 1867, was one of the main causes which damaged the reputation of the mines to such a degree that the country was nearly ruined by the reaction."

But it wasn't just process mania that debilitated the district. Expenses continued to rise, brought on by a terrible, enduring drought in the fall of 1863, followed by raging floods the next spring. War–spurred inflation dried up the sources of eastern money, and Indian attacks disrupted the already expensive shipping across the plains. Perhaps most importantly, many companies found they had severely over–capitalized their mines by buying expensive, unproven machinery that never worked.

## THE CROSBY & THOMPSON PROCESS

The Crosby & Thompson process was one of many sold throughout Gilpin County that claimed to remove sulfur from rich ores. In reality, the process did very little except relieve mine owners of much–needed cash. The process depended on a long, rotating, perforated cylinder. Operators placed gold ore inside, heated it, and then amalgamated it with mercury. Rossiter Raymond had some choice words about the process:

> This process was adopted by some thirty companies, and failed in every instance to effect a complete desulphurization. It was probably the most ruinous of the many experiments tried in the Territory, since so many parties risked so much capital upon it before its value had been sufficiently proved.

The inventors blamed poor gold recovery on a baseless theory that the gold somehow oxidized in large quantities during heating. They claimed that the gold was somehow blown out of the furnace as a brown powder. They eventually claimed to have "solved the problem," but oddly, none of their previous victims believed them. Raymond went on to comment:

> This discovery of the oxide of gold, by the way, was professedly made, not in the amalgamator, but in a very old book. Inventors would probably do better, in studying chemical subjects with which they are not thoroughly acquainted, to take modern instead of ancient literature as a guide.

As you might have guessed, the brown powder was a hoax, too.

It was common in Colorado mining for companies to build mills on the thinnest evidence of gold. Companies often built mills before a mine was even known to contain gold. Throughout Gilpin County, managers erected large, untested mills with stockholders' money on the fallacious premise that any technology that worked in California would also work in Colorado. Samuel Bowles observed in *The Switzerland of America* that

> This is why thousands of mines are unworked to–day; why scores of mills with unperfected processes, or plain stamps, stand idle, rotting and rusting in all parts of the territory; and why deserted cabins and vacant villages lie scattered in all the valleys about, —telling their tragic tales of loss and disappointment, monuments of the enthusiasm and credulity of miners and capitalists who labored and invested wildly before their time.

By April 1864, a combination of growing bad news from the mines and the financial effects of the Civil War caused Colorado mining stocks to collapse on the eastern exchanges. The collapse, though, didn't have as disastrous an effect in Colorado as it could have, had it happened a year sooner.

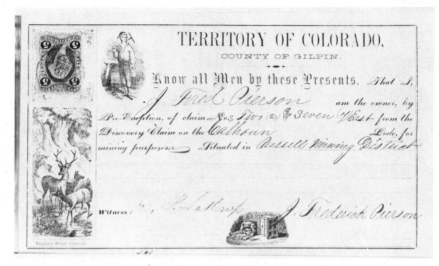

An 1867 preemptive deed for two claims on the Calhoun lode, west of Russell Gulch.—*Courtesy American West Archives, Cedar City, Utah.*

Mining, although terribly depressed for technical and financial reasons, had become more efficient out of sheer necessity. Local promoters, familiar with the district, knew there was a tremendous amount of gold still left in the mountains. They kept right on speculating in spite of the stock collapse, and mine ownership gradually shifted back to the West.

In 1865, Gilpin County gold production fell to 70,000 ounces, and it was only half that large a year later. It seemed that the only money to be made in the district was in the selling of properties. Wheeling and dealing became a way of life for the next few years. Hollister acridly commented, "So long as there is a market for mining property, it is incontestable that people will sell rather than work it."

Had this situation continued, Central City and Black Hawk would have eventually dried up and blown away like so many other ghost towns. As it was, the towns lost thousands of men to new gold finds elsewhere. It seemed that people were just holding on, waiting for some sign of good news. Fortunately, good news was visible on the horizon in the visage of Nathaniel Hill.

## Nathaniel P. Hill

Like Gregory before him, Hill turned out to be single-handedly responsible for creating uncountable wealth for the Central City area. Unlike his predecessor, though, Hill had staying power. He took advantage of his talent and vision.

At the time of his first visit in 1864, Nathaniel Hill was thirty-two years old and a professor at Brown University in Providence, Rhode Island. Acting as a scientific consultant, he came to assess the mineral potential of a large tract of land in southern Colorado. While in the territory, Hill visited Central City a number of times and apparently caught a case of gold fever. By 1865, he had

Nathaniel Hill and his family around 1865 or 1866, probably shortly before they moved to Central City.—*Photo by Coleman B. Remington, Providence, R.I. Courtesy of the Colorado Historical Society.*

formed two separate mining endeavors in Colorado, and both yielded fairly well before they encountered the ubiquitous sulfides.

Being a learned man, and one of the few real professors in the area, Hill was hired by James Lyon to help evaluate the potential for smelting near Black Hawk. Although Hill had no real operating knowledge of smelting, he nonetheless knew the rudiments of the technology. And he knew how to find out more.

With all due fanfare, Lyon fired up his furnaces in 1866 and smelted a large amount of high-quality ore as a test. To his chagrin, though, the test yielded little gold and was adjudged a failure by all involved. Like Burdsall before him, Lyon thoroughly gave up on the idea of smelting and never opened his plant for business.

As it turned out, Lyon's experiment was not really the failure he and others thought it had been at the time. In fact, the furnace had been poorly built by unskilled workers. During the test, it had leaked about half of the molten gold, silver, and copper into the underlying soil. The mistake was not found for several years, and by that time, Hill's star had already risen.

After working with Lyon, Hill became increasingly enamored with the idea of smelting. Unlike others, Hill recognized the potential for tremendous wealth. He knew that wealth would go to the first person who could actually perfect the process and successfully reopen the mines.

Hill returned to Providence and researched smelting technology through the fall of 1865. With study, he decided that the closest analogy to Gilpin County gold ores anywhere in the world was probably to be found in Wales. So he sailed to southern Wales and visited the smelting works at Swansea. He found the process very promising and returned to Central City the next spring.

Next, he tested his idea by purchasing seventy tons of high-grade ore from the Bobtail lode and shipping it over 7,000 miles to Swansea by wagon, barge, and boat.

Hill's experiment was very costly, but also wonderfully successful. As soon as he found the Swansea process worked, he rallied financial backing from his moneyed friends in the East. By May of 1867, he had officially incorporated the Boston & Colorado Smelting Company and promptly started building a new Swansea-style smelter at Black Hawk. Wisely, Hill hired experienced masons from Wales, and thus ensured expert construction of his furnaces. He next sought out a knowledgeable metallurgist and found Richard Pearce working in the nearby Empire District. With Pearce as his cornerstone, Hill founded his empire on solid technical ground and was ready for action.

Hill's smelting plant at Black Hawk was a small version of the Welsh plant he had seen the year before. The prototype plant at Swansea, however, employed both a smelting operation and a refinery. Hill apparently reasoned that the ores around Black Hawk would be exhausted in twenty or thirty years and decided that a refinery was just too expensive to build. Instead, he built the smelter by itself and used its furnaces to drive off the majority of sulfur and impurities. This produced a dense matte concentrate of copper, gold, and silver. Although the shipping costs were horrendous, he chose to ship the concentrated matte all the way to Wales for refining. For price protection, he signed a five-year

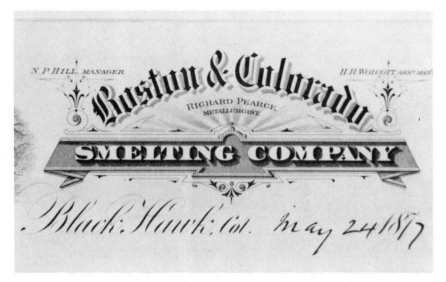

Note Pearce's prominent position on this 1877 letterhead from the Boston & Colorado Smelting Company.—*Courtesy American West Archives, Cedar City, Utah.*

contract to have the Swansea plant do the final separation of the precious metals.

Hill fired up his company's furnaces for experiments in June of 1867, and the while district watched in avid anticipation. Word of his unqualified success quickly spread across the district, and by fall, mines were readied for reopening. The Boston & Colorado plant became fully operational in January 1868, and the district was poised for its unbridled heyday.

## Rejuvenation

The rebirth had begun. In 1868, the first year of the plant's operation, gold production leaped to 79,000 ounces, and it almost doubled the following year. In 1870, Raymond wrote, "This year marks the new era of mining in Colorado. The old spirit of idleness and speculation has passed away. The new spirit of labor and economy has sprung into power."

The rate at which the mines reopened was incredible. Within three years, Gilpin County gold production topped 156,000 ounces for an all-time record that would never be surpassed. The health of Gilpin County gold mines and Hill's smelter were inextricably linked until the early 1880s. That is not to say there weren't problems.

For instance, the smelter used great quantities of firewood, and the nearby hillsides had already been stripped bare. The cost of importing wood was high, and that helped drive smelting costs up. Transportation costs for all commodities were expensive. Miners complained that Hill's $20 to $45 per ton smelting charges were exorbitant. The sulfur pollution around Black Hawk was terrible and would never be tolerated today. All the problems, however, were accepted as the price of progress.

Wagons hauling ore to the Boston & Colorado smelter. From a woodcut in *Harpers Weekly*, May 30, 1874.—*Courtesy Western History Department, Denver Public Library.*

Hill's 1868 successes caused renewed investment in the district. Standard–guage rail lines from the north and east reached Denver in the summer of 1870. By September of that year, rails were laid to Golden. Shipping costs dropped significantly and fell further when the narrow–gauge line of the Colorado Central reached Black Hawk in 1872.

There was a short–lived retreat as a recession hit the country in 1873 and gold production around Central City slackened. But just as it had a decade before, investment money soon reappeared for the glamorous Colorado gold mines, and the district recovered within a year or so. The railroads, on the other hand, found finances tight for years, and it was not until 1878 that the Colorado Central was able to complete its line to Central City.

Business had been good to Hill. In 1871, he opened a branch smelter in South Park to serve mines in the Como, Alma, and Fairplay districts. Growing all the while, his original plant attracted ores from Idaho Springs and Boulder County, even though transportation costs were staggering. With the advantage of rail in 1872, the Boston & Colorado smelter started taking ores from farther and farther afield.

The newly formed Denver Smelting Company built a smelter north of Denver in 1873 and situated it to take advantage of rail and nearby coal reserves. Moreover, there was a lot of open land. The new competition didn't adversely affect Hill, though, because the Denver plant was based on lead smelting technology while the Black Hawk plant survived on copper smelting techniques. The two plants used different techniques and smelted different ores.

By this time, Hill's refining contract with the Welsh refinery was due to expire, and he needed to extend it. However, the Swansea refinery wanted to raise its prices, and Hill could ill afford to raise his already expensive rates any

1877 view of the Boston & Colorado smelter on the company's letterhead. While the company was not necessarily proud of the pollution it caused, the billowing smokestacks were the symbol of American industry.—*Courtesy American West Archives, Cedar City, Utah.*

## VEGETATION

When prospectors first rushed into the mountains in the spring of 1859, they found lush forests of pine, cottonwood, and spruce. By September, though, the rabid rush for gold had wrecked the placid scene. In their search for placer gold, miners had turned most of the creeks upside-down. They had stripped practically all the hills around Central City bare for firewood, lumber, and mine timbers. By the spring of the following year, the forest devastation began spreading outward.

Many of the old photographs in this book show vignettes of the destruction. Looking at the hills today, though, it's hard to imagine how bad it really was. Here are Rossiter Raymond's comments in 1870:

> I desire to call attention particularly to one of the worst abuses attendant upon the settlement of the mining regions and other portions of the West. I allude to the wanton destruction of timber... Lumber has to be brought from twenty to forty miles, and heavy mill timbers often much further. And to obtain these articles, they are robbing and skinning districts that may at any day require their own timber just as much as Central City ever did... The question arises, "Where will this all end?"

His answer came a half century later when mining finally withered away around Central City.

higher. Driven to desperation, Richard Pearce finally devised a secret chemical method to extract gold and silver at the Black Hawk facility without an expensive refinery. Smelting charges went down instead of up.

By 1876, when Colorado was admitted to the union as the thirty–eighth state, commerce was booming. Competition in the smelting business heightened when three new plants were built at Golden in the mid–1870s. Golden seemed ideally situated between the Gilpin County gold frields and Boulder and Weld County coal fields. However, transportation costs for both commodities must have been too high, for the plants only worked a short time. Data on the subject is obscure, but it seems there may also have been insurmountable technical problems with the smelters themselves.

The Boston & Colorado Smelting Company works at Black Hawk.—*Photograph by Charles Weitfle of Central City. Courtesy Western History Department, Denver Public Library.*

By 1877, when there seemed to be more and more business coming from outside Central City, fuel had become an extreme problem for the Black Hawk smelter. Wood had become very expensive, and the federal government filed a lawsuit against the plant's use of wood from public lands. Even with rail service to the front door, it was still prohibitively expensive to ship coal up from the plains.

The smelter had also grown and was severely cramped in the narrow valley at Black Hawk. It could no longer expand to meet new demand for its services. In light of all these problems, Hill decided—and quickly convinced his eastern backers—to construct a new plant northwest of Denver. He wanted the new plant to be large, modern, and able to serve all of Colorado as well as other eastern states. He built his new "Argo" plant during 1878, fired it up in January 1879, and promptly closed the Black Hawk smelter that same year.

Gold production in the districts around Central City continued to rise, partly as a consequence of cheaper smelting rates and partly as a result of new milling developments. Research in the stamp mills during the late 1870s had proven that if the ore was crushed almost to the consistency of talcum powder, the mills could recover more gold than ever before. As the mills switched over to new stamps, mine owners found they could save money by sending only the richest portions of their ores to the smelter. Since money saved was money earned, the mines prospered.

## "ARGO"

"Argo" and "argonaut" were popular words in the 1800s, especially around the western gold fields. They need some elaboration today. The origin seems to stem from the Greek word *argos* meaning "bright, swift, glancing." It's gold field usage is nestled in Greek mythology with Jason's search for the Golden Fleece on his ship the *Argo* with his fearless band of "argonauts." Many popular accounts of the era referred to the California-bound Forty-niners as "argonauts," and the term resurfaced ten years later in Colorado.

## Silver Discoveries

After great silver discoveries were made at Leadville in 1877, silver prospecting picked up all over the state. In the spring of 1878, S.W. Tyler and E.A. Lynn found a rich silver vein north of Black Hawk that had somehow eluded searchers for almost twenty years. There ensued a small rush of claiming and silver mining on the flanks of Silver Hill. The deposits, however, were nowhere near as rich as the miners and stockholders had hoped, and the mines quickly played out. Silver production, nonetheless, climbed to the lofty level of 232,000 ounces in 1879.

A view looking northeast toward the Boston & Colorado smelter shortly after it moved to the "Argo" suburb of Denver. The large buildings just outside the compound were part of the Argo Hotel. An industrial complex just north of the intersection of Interstate Highways 70 and 25 now covers the site.—*Courtesy Western History Department, Denver Public Library.*

## The Air Drill

In the mid–1870s, inventors devised several varieties of mechanical drills that promised to make underground gold mining both easier and cheaper. Powered at first by steam and later by compressed air, drills worked much faster than men, with only a fraction of the effort. Companies with large payrolls liked the new tool, but there was considerable resistance to it among the miners. Economics, nonetheless, won out, and the companies gradually replaced hundreds of experienced hand–drillers with mechanical drills.

As unfortunate as it seemed at the time, the luckiest miners were actually those who lost their drilling jobs. (Many drillers switched occupations and took to sharpening the drill steels dulled by the new machinery.) The drill was so powerful that it literally ground the rock to a fine powder and blew the dust out in a dense cloud for the operator to breathe. It usually took only a few years of such abuse before many of the "lucky" miners who had kept their drilling jobs died with racking coughs, seemingly unable to breathe.

In autopsies, doctors commonly ascribed their deaths to "miner's

Double jacking. One man held the drill steel and the other swung the hammer. The scene is too cramped, so the people were probably posing for photographer Lachlan McLean.—*Courtesy Western History Collections, University of Colorado.*

consumption" or "miners asthma" (a lung disease known today as silicosis). While survivors filed numerous lawsuits against companies that used the so-called widow-maker drills, almost none were successful.

For twenty years, miners, drill manufacturers, and mining companies tried to find ways to keep the choking dust under control. Finally, in the late 1890s, a Denver inventor devised a method to pump a mist of water through the middle of drill steels. This finally controlled the dust problem, and as the drills were modified, deaths from the widow-makers tapered off.

Knowing this, you can roughly date many mining photographs by looking at the mechanical rock drill. If you can see only one hose connected to a drill, that hose carried compressed air or steam, and the drill was a widow-maker. If you can see two hoses in the picture, one carried water, and the drill was made or modified sometime after 1897.

This was the Oliver Mill in Chase Gulch west of Black Hawk, with a part of the Bonanza Mill showing at the left.—*Courtesy Western History Department, Denver Public Library.*

With separate hoses for air and water, this drill was much safer than the earlier widow-maker models because it didn't create so much dust.—*Photograph by Lachlan McLean. Courtesy Western History Collections, University of Colorado.*

With the air drill wedged between the walls, this miner was preparing to blast ore out of the roof. The drill he was using created heavy clouds of rock dust and anyone who used the drill for long developed "miner's consumption," or silicosis. Until the dust problem was solved in the late 1890s, the drill deserved its popular name, the widow–maker.—*Courtesy Western History Department, Denver Public Library.*

# Gilpin Tramway

Like Hill's smelter, companies built most of the large mills along Clear Creek near Black Hawk to take advantage of water power. That meant that the mines had to haul their ore, in some cases for several miles, down the hills and valleys to Black Hawk. Wagon haulage, however, was expensive. Investors finally initiated a plan for cheap rail transportation in the fall of 1886 and dubbed it the Gilpin Tramway. As expected, the teamsters strongly opposed the railroad because they weren't willing to give up their lucrative hauling businesses.

But the miners wanted the rail. Over teamster objections, the Gilpin Tramway was laid as a tightly twisting, two–foot–gauge rail line north from Black Hawk a short distance up Clear Creek. At the northern boundary of town, it turned west, and after many switchbacks, gained enough altitude to reach Central City. From there, it wound upward to the top of Quartz Hill south of Nevadaville, then south to Russell Gulch, and ultimately to mines in the southern part of the county.

As the miners had hoped, it cost less to ship ore by rail. In retrospect, though, the tramway undercharged for its service. Although it operated for thirty–one years, it never turned much of a profit. Nonetheless, it lowered shipping costs sufficiently so that a number of mines could stay in business in the face of declining reserves.

The Colorado & Southern Railroad bought the tramway in 1906 and operated it as the Gilpin Railroad until 1917. All of its twenty–one miles of track are now gone, but parts of its bed remain if one knows where to look.

An undated, but very early, photograph of the Bonanza Mill by G.R. Appel of Denver. This mill was situated near the head of Chase Gulch west of Black Hawk.—*Courtesy Western History Department, Denver Public Library.*

# The Good Times

Smelter competition continued to grow through the 1880s. The Grant smelter was built at Globeville, north of Denver, in 1882, followed by the Globe smelter nearby in 1886. Many mines in the Central City area had run out of near-surface ore and were having to go to record depths for gold. While not all of the mines maintained good gold values at depth, production hovered around 60,000 to 100,000 ounces of gold per year. Silver production followed a similar path, with production ranging from 100,000 to 300,000 ounces per year throughout the decade.

In the years after the Civil War, the country experienced a prolonged deflationary period, and the buying power of the dollar grew to an all-time high. When combined with the overall cheapening of goods in the Central City District, precious metal mining stayed lucrative.

From 1886 to 1917, the two-foot-gauge Gilpin Tramway was instrumental in getting ore cheaply from the mines to the mills. This receipt, dated 1912, which was after the line was renamed the Gilpin Railway, shows a one-car shipment from the Saratoga mine to the Polar Star mill. *Author's Collection.*

In 1893, however, a number of complicated national and global factors combined to drive the price of silver drastically downward, culminating in the "Silver Crash" that year. Although the monstrous silver–producing districts of Leadville and Aspen were decimated, Central City and the rest of Gilpin County fared quite well. In Gilpin County, silver was essentially a by–product of gold extraction, and few mines were solely dependent upon silver.

Metal extraction had grown more efficient throughout the 1880s and 1890s, but slow, subtle changes were underway. At Hill's smelter there was a growing shortage of the copper–rich gold ores the plant had been designed to use. Mines around Central City had been dug deeper and deeper, but the veins were poorer at depth than they had been near the surface.

Water had become a significant, ever–increasing problem. Only a few mines could afford the large pumps they needed to lift water to the surface. The water problem grew worse as mines were linked underground. It became obvious that if one mine were allowed to shut down and flood, all the connected mines would have to follow suit.

Again, a number of related events worked to keep the backbone of mining strong in the Central City area. First came the refinement of the miner's air drill in 1897. Then, in 1899, the huge American Smelting and Refining Company (ASARCO) was organized, and it quickly acquired practically every smelter in the state. By near–monopolistic consolidation, ASARCO closed most of the state's small and less efficient plants and managed to make smelting more economical.

To be sure, cheaper drilling and cheaper smelting helped those mines that were still open around the turn of the century. A lot of mines, though, had already closed because of water problems. What could be done for them?

## The Argo or Newhouse Tunnel

Regardless of commodity, mining has always faced two costly problems: the removal of ore and the removal of water. Even from the earliest days of 1859, those two problems were responsible for more mine failures than all other causes put together.

# WATER-FILLED MINES

It was never cheap keeping a mine dry even when finding gold was easy. As soon as the gold gave out, or as soon as it cost too much to get the gold out, the miners walked away. They abandoned their mine and left it to fill with water.

As the abandoned mine flooded, water would start seeping into nearby working mines. Often, seepage became overwhelming and forced even rich mines to shut down. The domino effect of mine flooding periodically left the whole area dotted with huge underground reservoirs.

When possible, miners blasted horizontal tunnels into the hillsides to act as giant water drains. Although there were many such tunnels. the largest and most successful drainage tunnel in the region was the Argo Tunnel. After almost eighty years, it still drains mines all the way from Idaho Springs to Nevadaville.

There were many underground connections between the mines, and the connections made drainage more complicated. Often miners could not drain even one small, insignificant mine without draining many others. By 1900, the oldest mines were abandoned and the amount of water stored underground became almost unimaginable.

It was also dangerous. In 1895, miners drilling deep underground in the Americus mine, near Black Hawk, accidentally hit an unmapped section of the Fisk mine. The rock wall between the two mines suddenly burst from the colossal force of the impounded water. Twelve miners died instantly in the Americus mine. Two more perished when the flood waters raced through underground connections into the nearby Sleepy Hollow mine.

The circumstances of the Americus disaster were repeated in the Argo Tunnel on January 19, 1943. Four miners were drilling and blasting in the lowest sections of the Kansas mine, 3.6 miles from the portal. Although the mine had been draining into the tunnel for over thirty years, the miners accidentally hit a portion of the mine still filled with water. Water flooded over them, killing all, and closed the tunnel for good.

There are unmapped sections of mines in practically every district in the country. That's the rule, not the exception. What is surprising, though, is that there were only two such major catastrophes in a century of mining around Central City.

By the 1880s, people familiar with the deep Gilpin County mines knew the district would fail without economical water drainage. Water pumps were primitive, and operators had to literally bail the water out of many mines with buckets. There were a few horizontal drainage tunnels in the district, and they

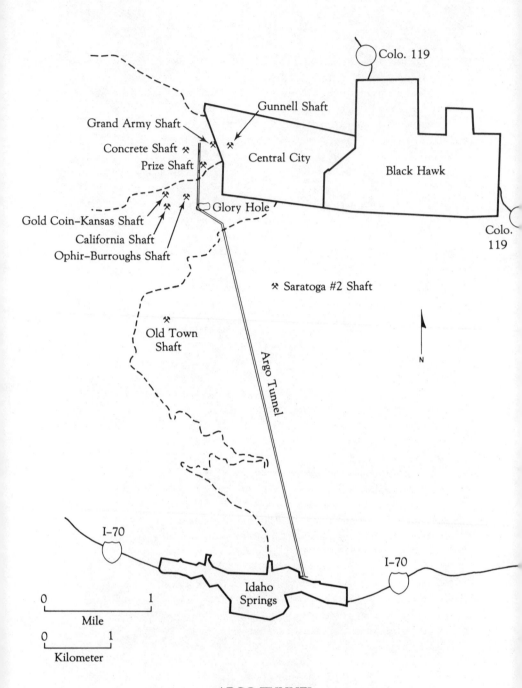

**ARGO TUNNEL**

Map showing the relationship of the Argo Tunnel to surface features.

North

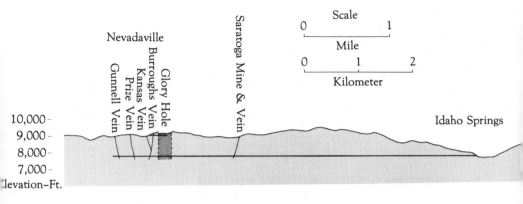

ARGO TUNNEL—SIDE VIEW

Cross section through the mountains from Idaho Springs to
Nevadaville showing the Argo Tunnel and several major veins.

provided relief for a few shallow mines, but deep mines that extended below
creek levels were in real trouble.

Observers knew that Clear Creek at Idaho Springs was almost a thousand
feet lower than Central City. It was over two thousand feet lower than the rich
mines on Quartz Hill near Nevadaville. Therefore, if some company could dig
a drainage tunnel under the mountains from Idaho Springs, it could drain
much of the gold district. While a number of tunnel companies were organized
to accomplish that task, only one had enough money to turn the dream into
reality.

Ground was broken for the Newhouse Tunnel (almost immediately
renamed, and known today as the Argo Tunnel) late in 1893. The intent of the
project was really twofold: (1) to drive a large drainage tunnel from Idaho
Springs under the mountains toward Nevadaville, and (2) to access gold veins
at great depths below the surface.

Although it took sixteen years to dig, the tunnel certainly achieved its goals.
By 1910, when the tunnel reached its maximum length of 4.16 miles, it had
directly or indirectly drained probably a hundred large and small mines. At
Nevadaville, the Argo Tunnel was about 1,300 feet deep and is now one of the
major reasons you'll see little surface water flowing down nearby creeks today.

Although the Argo Tunnel was dug both for mining and for drainage, it was
much more successful for the latter than it was for mining. While the tunnel
cut numerous gold veins, most were not particularly rich at the tunnel level.
Moreover, many of the mines around Central City hoisted ore out their own
shafts instead of hauling the ore through the tunnel to Idaho Springs.
Nonetheless, some sources estimate that as much as $100 million in ore may
have been shipped out the tunnel during its fifty year life.

The project was huge and costly, but it was a money–maker. Throughout the first two and a half miles, the tunnel was twelve feet wide by twelve feet high; beyond, it dropped to nine to ten feet wide by six feet high. The operation used electric locomotives to haul ore out of the tunnel and about half of the tunnel had two sets of railroad tracks.

Much of the tunnel's financial success hinged on ore haulage and the large Argo Mill built in 1913. Ore production was substantial in the early years, but production dropped off as the mines in Gilpin County were depleted. Although the mill continued to work for a while, all activity through the tunnel stopped when an accidental flood and cave–in clogged it in 1943. (You can still visit the mill at Idaho Springs and get a rare, first–hand idea of what milling was like.)

With the success of the Argo Tunnel, several other grandiose schemes were planned from time to time to help drain other flooded and idle producers. The Argo, however, was the only really successful effort, because, realistically, the district had already passed middle age. Too many mines were played out and tunneling was very expensive.

That is not to say there was no gold left. It was just very expensive to find and extract. An engineer named George Collins assessed the problem in the September 1910 issue of the *Mining and Scientific Press*: Further exploration (in Gilpin County) is . . . handicapped by the great expense of unwatering before a stroke of work can be done toward the opening of new ground."

Central City's mining days were numbered.

A view deep within the Argo Tunnel. The right–hand branch probably led to mine works on one of the many gold veins cut by the tunnel.—*Courtesy Western History Department. Denver Public Library.*

The great Argo Mill at Idaho Springs is still open for visitation, although it hasn't processed ore for many years. The date of this Denver Commercial Photo Company shot is unknown, but is probably of 1920s vintage.—*Courtesy Western History Department, Denver Public Library.*

View looking down on the town of Black Hawk and its Black Hawk mill (later owned by the Fifty Gold Mines Company). The date and photographer are unknown, but the photo was probably shot around 1900.—*Courtesy Western History Department, Denver Public Library.*

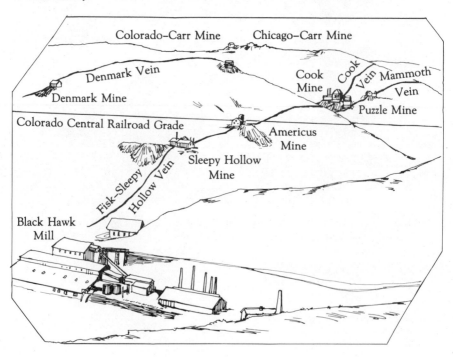

# The Decline

Crawford Hill took over the declining Boston & Colorado smelting business just before his father, Nathaniel, died in 1900. By that time, fewer and fewer mines were producing the copper–rich gold ores the plant needed. Then in 1909, a fire destroyed the refinery portion of the plant, so Crawford and the board of directors decided to close the plant the next year. That left only the Globe smelter for the convenient use of Gilpin County mines. If it had not been for the Argo Tunnel and the Argo Mill, the district might have suffered a death–blow then and there.

For the next few years, gold production from Central City mines leveled out at 35,000 to 40,000 ounces per year. In the long run, though, the mining business was on a decline.

By the beginning of World War I, gold production slipped to less than 20,000 ounces, and it continued to drop during the war. It was obvious the district would never recover. The point was cruelly underlined when the Colorado & Southern stopped its rail service to Central City in 1925.

A view of the office and part of the works of the Black Hawk mill. Although undated, this photograph was probably taken after 1900. The ore cars at the top of the mill probably came from the large Fifty Gold Mines operation at the Bobtail Tunnel.— *Courtesy Western History Department, Denver Public Library.*

# Jump to $35

In 1927, 69 years after gold was discovered in Gilpin County, production dropped to a new all-time low of only 1,300 ounces. In 1933, however, the government suspended its mandated price of gold. With the $20.67 per ounce price eliminated, gold sought its own global level. In 1934, the government again reinstituted price controls, this time at $35 per ounce, and mining around Central City made a short-lived comeback.

With the price of gold suddenly 69 percent higher than it had been only two years before, there was considerable impetus to reopen idle mines. Although underground mines in Gilpin County produced over 20,000 ounces of gold in 1935, all the old problems were still present. There was simply no way production could be sustained. Underground mining soon died again.

With the new higher price of gold, placer mining also staged a comeback. Using modern equipment, the Humphrey's Gold Corporation, and others that followed, removed more placer gold (69,000 ounces) in six years than had been mined in all the previous seventy-six.

Decline was nonetheless inevitable, and as mines depleted the placers, production again fell. Rail service to Black Hawk stopped in 1941, and then in 1943, the Argo Tunnel cave-in halted all production there.

Uranium prospecting reached a fever pitch across the West during the post-war 1950s, and miners discovered small amounts of uranium in a few of the Gilpin County gold veins. There was a slight uptick in gold production as miners removed some of the veins to search for uranium, but the district never again produced more than 600 ounces of gold per year.

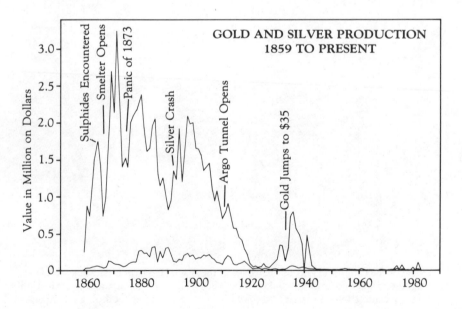

A 1918 view of the Gilpin-Eureka mine west of Central City. There was a short-lived spurt of activity at this mine during the 1950s search for uranium.—*Photo by the Denver Commercial Photo Co. Courtesy Western History Department, Denver Public Library.*

# New Forces

By 1968, the United States Congress and other free world governments realized that the $35 gold standard could not exist in the face of worldwide inflation. Governments desperately tried to maintain constant gold prices, but the gold market naturally developed a two-tier split between official prices and free-market prices. In 1972, the United States officially removed all gold backing from the dollar, and the price of gold stabilized at $50 to $100 per ounce. In 1974, with the threat of a prolonged Arab oil embargo, psychological and financial insecurity forced gold up to $150 per ounce. It maintained that level until 1977.

Global political forces, including problems in Iran and Afghanistan, coupled with rapid inflation of the dollar, drove the price of gold up to its all-time high of $852 per ounce in January 1980. At the same time, efforts by individuals to corner the silver market drove silver up to $48.80 per ounce. All across Colorado, mining suddenly took on a renewed glamour.

Central City, like other old districts, became the focus of vigorous activity, and "No Trespassing" signs appeared everywhere. As expected, though, gold was severely overpriced, and it soon fell back to roughly $500 per ounce. Owners of new and old claims found that even with gold prices at $500 an ounce, mines were still unprofitable.

Why? Except for the mines drained by the Argo Tunnel and other minor tunnels, all the old mines were flooded. And because of extensive underground interconnections, many abandoned mines would have to have been drained in order to rework just one. More importantly, most of the mines had long ago had their richest ores removed. When coupled with expensive 1970s labor costs, all the problems made the extraction of the remaining low-grade gold ore almost impossible.

## The Future

Numerous environmental protection laws have been enacted in the last two decades, and they effectively outlaw old-fashioned "rape and pillage" mining. No longer can one just buy a gold property and hope to start mining the next day. Miners must now acquire valid state and federal mining permits, which require, literally, volumes of official paperwork. Even mine drainage may be next to impossible, because stagnant mine waters are very acidic and there are strict legal restraints against discharging such pollution.

That's not to say there can't or won't be more mining around Central City in the future. There are certainly a few profitable opportunities just waiting for the right entrepreneur to develop. Large-scale mining, however, will probably demand a stable price of gold in the $800 to $900 an ounce range, and that seems unlikely in the next five to ten years.

Abandoned, and long forgotten, this machine guards a collapsed tunnel near Nevadaville.

—*Photo by Robert Hovermale.*

In this rare photograph, the gold–bearing vein, about a foot wide, shows up quite well just to the left of the miner's pick.—*Photo by Lachlan McLean. Courtesy Western History Collections, University of Colorado.*

# THE GEOLOGY OF GOLD

Gold was found around Central City in two settings: in vein deposits inside the mountains and in placer deposits in the valley bottoms.

## Veins

Around Central City, 99 percent of all the gold mined came from vein deposits. Veins are thin, curtain–like bodies of rock that cut through the hills. In some places, like around Central City, they contain gold or other valuable minerals. To picture what a vein looks like inside the earth, imagine a child's ant farm; the material between the two pieces of glass would be a vein. And much in the manner of the ants removing soil to build their colonies, miners dig shafts and tunnels through the vein to remove gold. Unlike an ant farm, though, veins are never uniform in orientation or width.

Like a curtain, veins often bend and twist along their length. They often intersect other veins and branch into roughly parallel veins that the miners call shoots. Most gold veins around Central City are tilted ten to twenty degrees away from vertical, and they vary from paper thin to over forty feet wide. If you'd like to see what a vein looks like in real life, drive 0.4 miles toward Central City from Highway 119. On your right you will see a slot where miners completely removed the Gregory vein from below the road level to high above you on the hillside.

It was always hard to locate and trace veins along the hillsides. Most rich veins were only a couple of feet wide, at best, and were usually covered with dirt and vegetation. It was much easier for miners to follow gold veins underground. Since they only advanced their workings a few feet per day, miners had time to closely examine the rocks they were drilling. Moreover, miners found that their veins normally looked more yellowish than the surrounding rocks. Whenever their veins split or joined other veins, the miners had to decide which branch seemed the richest one to follow.

Most gold veins were short. In the typical operation, miners could only follow a vein for a couple of hundred feet before it disappeared or became too poor to pursue. By the same token, most veins were only rich down to a couple of hundred feet. On the other hand, there were a few extraordinary veins that extended for one or two miles along the surface and were fairly rich down to 1,000 or 1,500 feet deep.

# Vein Formation

Gold–bearing veins were not formed along with the rest of the rocks that make up the surrounding hills. Instead, they were formed long afterward by the injection of hot water solutions into faults that cut through the older rocks.

A fault is merely a crack in the earth's surface where the rocks on either side have moved relative to one another. The rocks need not have moved much. For an everyday example, look at practically any structure made of concrete blocks. Do you see the cracks? They're always there somewhere. Those cracks are tiny faults. In each fault, one side has moved up, down, or sideways relative to the other, sometimes only fractions of an inch. You can see thousands of examples of these types of structural faults almost everywhere in sidewalks, driveways, and buildings. And just as these cracks commonly split into several branches, so do the faults in the earth's crust.

There are literally hundreds of small, long–dormant faults and fractures in the Central City area. Long ago, slow movements in the earth's crust forced rich chemical solutions into those cracks. The solutions came from deep within the earth and contained small amounts of gold, silver, lead, copper, and zinc carried along in large quantities of silica and sulfur. As the hot solutions cooled, minerals formed much in the manner that rock candy forms from hot sugar solutions.

Some of the vein deposits were extremely complicated with all sorts of branching, pinching, swelling, intersections, and barren zones. That is what the miners had to contend with every day. When neighboring miners couldn't clear up overlapping claims to various offshoots of a vein, they sued each other and the courts stepped in.

All through this book are references to ores and ore deposits. Simply put, ore zones are places along veins where valuable minerals are concentrated and can be profitably mined. The profit portion of the definition is very important. It means that the definition of ore constantly changes. It means that something classified as ore today might not be classified as ore tomorrow.

# Placers

As previously mentioned, many gold–bearing veins extend from deep within the earth all the way to the surface. The parts of the veins nearest the surface are subjected to the effects of water and oxygen for thousands of years, and they gradually disintegrate. Since gold is fairly insoluble, it stays behind as a myriad of particles while the surrounding rocks wash away. In time, rainstorms and melting snows carry the gold particles down the hillsides. In the gulches, the gold is mixed up with a random mishmash of sand, gravel, and boulders.

Gold is six to eight times as dense as most other pieces of sand and gravel, and any flood capable of moving debris downstream allows gold to quickly sink toward the bottom of the drainage. Over time, such processes allow gold to concentrate into rich zones in the creek gravels that miners and prospectors call placers. (Pronounced like "plaster" without the "t.")

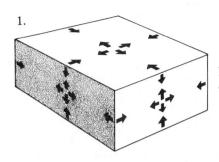

1.

Movements in the Earth's crust cause tremendous forces.

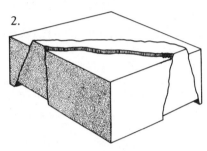

2.

Rocks in the Earth's crust break. The fractures are called faults.

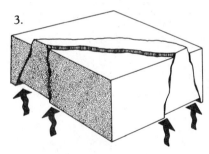

3.

Hot solutions rise from deep in the Earth's crust. Veins form as the solutions cool.

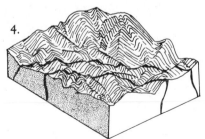

4.

The Earth's surface erodes. Over time, hills and valleys form.

**VEIN FORMATION**

51

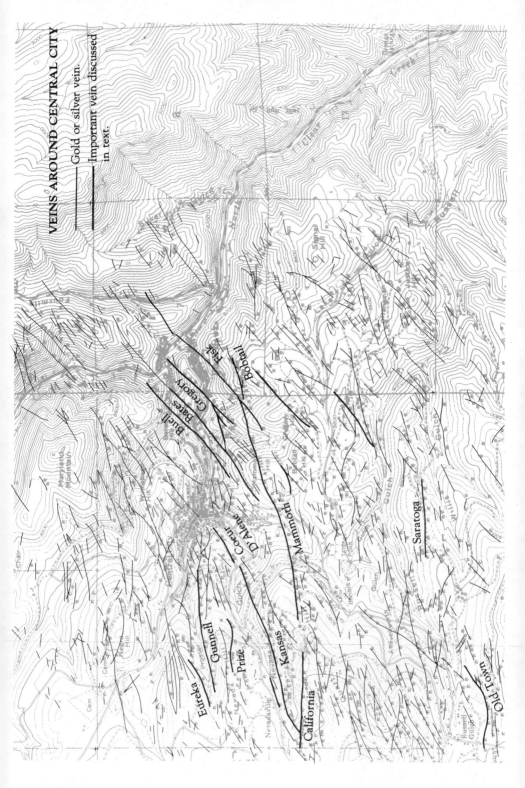

VEINS AROUND CENTRAL CITY

—— Gold or silver vein.

—— Important vein discussed in text.

Buell
Bates
Gregory
Fisk
Bobtail
Eureka
Gunnell
Prize
Coeur D'Alene
Kansas
Mammoth
California
Saratoga
Old Town

52

Depending on how far the placer is from the original vein, gold can occur either as a nugget, a flattened flake, or as finely ground flour. The prospector commonly referred to all forms of placer gold as "gold dust."

Early prospectors searched for placer deposits. That's what the Pikes Peak Gold Rush in 1859 was all about. And reasonably so, for prospectors could find placers fairly easily. Even greenhorns could find and work one without undue expense or experience. Moreover, any prospector worth his salt could prospect upstream from his placer, in a systematic manner, and have a good chance of finding where his gold dust came from.

The exact location of this photograph is unknown, but it's probably in one of the drainages around the Gregory Diggings. In *Colorado on Glass*, author Terry Mangan says photographer Rufus Cable shot this in either 1859 or 1860.—*Courtesy Western History Department, Denver Public Library.*

# Gold and Other Vein Minerals

Gold was found in two forms around Central City: as native gold and as gold telluride. Fortunately for the miners seeking quick fortunes, practically all of the Central City gold occurred in its easily recognizable, metallic form called native gold. Tellurides, on the other hand, are mineral combinations of gold and tellurium that bear no visual resemblance to the shiny, soft yellow metal that prospectors knew. (Tellurium is a silvery–white metal, and telluride minerals are usually brassy–yellow to silvery–white.)

Had there been much gold telluride around Central City, the early prospectors probably would have overlooked the area in 1859. In fact, they overlooked the gold telluride minerals in the famous Cripple Creek District until 1891. And that district ultimately produced four times the gold of Central City and Gilpin County.

Miners called high concentrations of gold "pay zones." You can see a pay zone here between the drill and the miner on the right side of the face.—*Photo by Lachlan McLean, Courtesy Western History Collections, University of Colorado.*

Native gold was generally disseminated throughout the ores in particles so small as to be invisible without a lens. It was rare for the underground miner to actually see gold streaks in his ore.

In its native form, gold is always naturally alloyed with silver and small amounts of other metals. As a consequence of gold mining, then, silver was extracted as a by-product of gold milling and smelting. Silver was an important commodity in its own right and even occurred occasionally in its native state. Normally, though, silver was chemically bound up in a number of other minerals. While there are a few silver-bearing veins in the Silver Hill area north of Black Hawk, the regions' silver deposits were neither as rich nor as profitable as its gold veins.

Gold and silver are known as precious metals. But much of the vein material around Central City also contained large amounts of base metals. When the ore was smelted, it was easy to recover some of the more valuable base metals like copper, lead, and zinc, and they helped add to the profit margin. Base metal production began with copper in 1868, lead in 1873, and zinc in 1885.

A handful of mines also contained small amounts of uranium, and its discovery spawned a small flurry of activity in the cold-war era of the 1950s. Uranium mining, however, never attained much economic importance, and the little uranium that was produced came from old gold mines.

## Some Facts About Gold

Since completely pure gold never occurs in nature, and since gold is so valuable, people who routinely work with gold have devised two ways to express gold purity. Jewelers use one system and practically everyone else uses the other.

You've certainly come across the jewelers' system when you've seen rings and necklaces labeled as 18-carat, 20K or the like. K is the abbreviation for carat, and pure gold is 24-carat gold. However, pure gold is too soft to be worn as jewelry, so gold is alloyed with copper and silver to make it harder. For instance, 22-carat gold is an alloy of twenty-two parts gold, one part silver, and one part copper.

Miners, smelters, industries, and commodity traders rely on a different, more precise measure of purity referred to as fineness. Pure gold is determined to be 1000 fine and has no impurities. Because it's difficult to refine pure gold in large quantities, most commerce uses 999 fine gold as its standard.

The purity of the gold mined around Central City and Black Hawk varies considerably, but generally ranges from about 700 to 860 fine. This means that gold samples actually contain from 70 percent to 86 percent pure gold; most of the rest is silver. With the world market price of pure gold hovering in the $450 per ounce range, any impure gold you pick up in the hills around Central City today is probably worth from $320 to $390 per ounce.

Jewelers sell gold by the pennyweight, but practically everyone else sells it by the ounce. Gold and other precious metals are measured in Troy ounces, whereas typical commodities like groceries are measured in avoirdupois ounces. Troy ounces are almost 10 percent heavier: one Troy ounce equals 1.097 avoirdupois ounces.

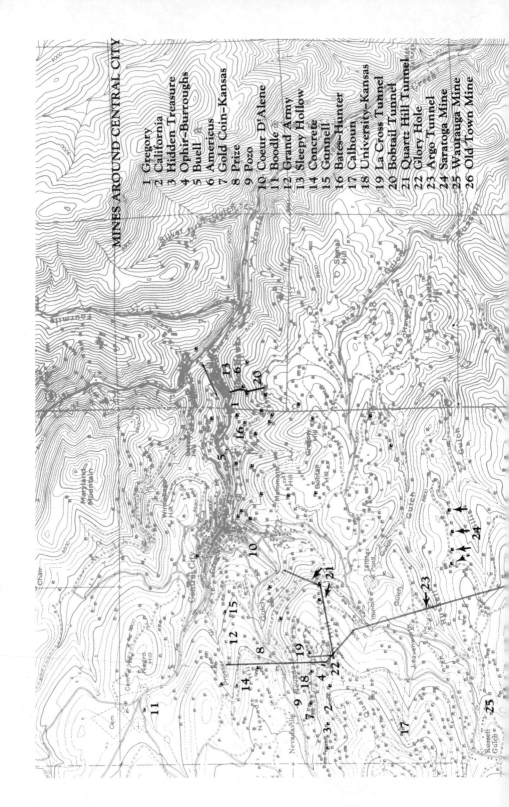

MINES AROUND CENTRAL CITY

1 Gregory
2 California
3 Hidden Treasure
4 Ophir–Burroughs
5 Buell
6 Americus
7 Gold Coin–Kansas
8 Prize
9 Pozo
10 Coeur D'Alene
11 Boodle
12 Grand Army
13 Sleepy Hollow
14 Concrete
15 Gunnell
16 Bates–Hunter
17 Calhoun
18 University–Kansas
19 La Cross Tunnel
20 Bobtail Tunnel
21 Quartz Hill Tunnel
22 Glory Hole
23 Argo Tunnel
24 Saratoga Mine
25 Wautauga Mine
26 Old Town Mine

# MINES

It's hard to imagine how much sweat and nitroglycerin the old–time miners invested in the ground around Central City. Every hole you see there now remains as an aging visual testament to some miner's dream. And many of those dreams were failures. In his 1921 book, *Grown Gold*, Peter McFarlane reflected, "On the one hand, we had youth, muscle and vigor to aid in producing results. On the other, little sense, less money, and no experience; surely a trinity of worthless assets."

Miners named most of the holes you see in the hills around town. Many of the names still survive on old claim records and in newspapers. Connecting names and locations, however, is difficult and often impossible. In the early 1960s, a government geologist named Paul Sims made the best effort so far at cataloging old mines around Central City. With his coauthors, Sims found about 2,500 shafts, tunnels, and prospect pits in the small area covered in this book. He was able to attach names to only about 620 of them. He never intended to be exhaustive, and the actual number of prospects probably tops 5,000.

The typical mine was small. It usually employed only a handful of miners and worked for only a few months. A few years at most. Even the largest, most profitable operations produced on a sporadic schedule. George Collins, a Gilpin County mining engineer, commented in 1910 that "The output for two generations has been remarkably steady, but when we come down to the individual mines, we find few of them have been in operation continuously for more than eight or ten years at most."

This on/off flow of production made accurate record–keeping difficult. Record–keeping was seldom important to independent miners during the 1860s anyway. Few kept records, and when they did, they kept them secret. Since record–keeping was inaccurate, today's estimation of gold production for any mine, or group of mines, is educated guesswork.

Finding mine maps is even more difficult. Like production records, owners usually kept their maps as guarded secrets. Some of the ones included in this book are available only because someone shared them with government geologists many years ago. Others survive in libraries and are now one–of–a–kind items. Most maps, however, are probably lost. Contrary to popular opinion, there is no vast repository of old mine maps.

If you're one of the many people who find mine maps hard to understand, you're not alone. Go back to a previous analogy, though, and try to imagine the maps as drawings of huge underground ant farms. The patterned areas are where miners removed gold ore. (Some of today's large mines make three–dimensional models out of clear plastic to get around the visualization problem.)

Most Central City mines share several common attributes. The veins were

## MILLS

With all their odd–looking, noisy machinery, mills seemed like three–dimensional jigsaw puzzles. Workers dumped ore in hoppers at the top of the plant and carried out gold concentrates from the bottom. What happened in between seemed mysterious.

Actually, mills used a number of relatively simple processes to get at the gold. Near the top of the typical mill were crushers that broke large chunks of ore into smaller pieces. Pumps added water, and the ore fell down chutes to the stamp mills. There, the repeated dropping of heavy iron pistons crushed the ore into a fine, wet powder.

Below the stamps came amalgamation, and that process varied from mill to mill. Regardless of the machinery, crushed ore was mixed with mercury, and the gold and silver stuck to it. The rest of the powdered rock floated off and was discarded outside the mill onto the tailings pile. Next, workers gathered up the gold/silver/mercury alloy, known as amalgam, and heated it in a special iron container. There, the heat drove off the mercury. Left behind was a porous piece of gold and silver called sponge, that was then weighed, assayed, and eventually sold to the U.S. Mint.

Certain ores were resistant to amalgamation. In those ores, the gold and silver wouldn't stick to the mercury and would wash completely through the mill. For such ores, the mill operators replaced the amalgamation process and with a form of concentration. That process depended on a vibrating table that concentrated the valuable material like a gold pan. Operators then sent the concentrate to a smelter.

In the 1890s, engineers discovered that a cyanide solution would dissolve gold and silver right out of the ores. Moreover, the cyanide solution gave up the precious metals quite easily through chemical means. Even today, the cyanide process is still among the cheapest and most efficient methods of getting gold out of low–grade ores.

usually very rich and highly profitable near the surface. They grew less profitable at depth. Water problems also became severe at depth, and only large companies could afford to pump out deep operations. Throughout the 1850s and 1860s, prospectors divided the veins into 100-foot claims. From about 1862 on, companies gradually combined the small claims into larger units, and small mines lost their separate identities.

The mines described here were some of the most important, or most visible, mines in the district. The list is far from exhaustive. If you would like to know more about the hundreds of mines not listed here, check the references at the end of the book.

## Bates Vein

Even before the gold rush really got rolling at full steam, John Gregory was already a busy character. Somehow he took time from his sluices to prospect, and in doing so, he found a second vein on May 19, 1859. Of course, he didn't have to go far. His second discovery was only 1,000 feet up Gregory Gulch from his original strike. Gregory named the new lode in honor of Captain W. H. Bates, a member of the DeFreese party of Indiana miners.

Richer parts of the Bates sometimes yielded two ounces of gold per man per day, although the gold occurred in unpredictable pockets. The vein was usually about five feet wide, but it occasionally widened to twenty feet in spots. The Bates probably yielded as much as 115,000 ounces of gold and 725,000 ounces of silver.

Mining on the Bates was especially intense during the first few years before the shafts hit the sulfides. After a period of inactivity in the mid-1860s, mining restarted on the Bates, but it never seemed to regain its former glory.

There were many shafts on the Bates dating back to 1859. Most of the activity was centered near Gregory Gulch, about where the present road into Central City branches into its two one-way sections. The vein split into smaller shoots at its south end, and the gold content tapered off toward the north end of the vein. The silver content increased to the north, however, and there was a short-lived flurry of mining activity on the north end of the vein in the late 1870s.

In 1988, a modern company began extensive rehabilitation work on the Bates vein, and that activity is welcomed as a major new investment in the historic district. You'll see the new headframe, buildings, and equipment just south of the blacktop road to Central City. If successful, the mine may soon yield valuable ore from over 900 feet deep.

## Bobtail Vein

Discovered during the early days of the 1859 gold rush, the Bobtail was named in honor of a bobtailed ox. Like most other lodes, the ore from near the surface was very, very rich. It's doubtful, though, that it was rich enough to warrant the following quote from the December 30, 1862, edition of the *Central City Tri-Weekly Mining Life*: "The Bobtail has become the greatest gold property on the continent, and is known as the Comstock of Colorado."

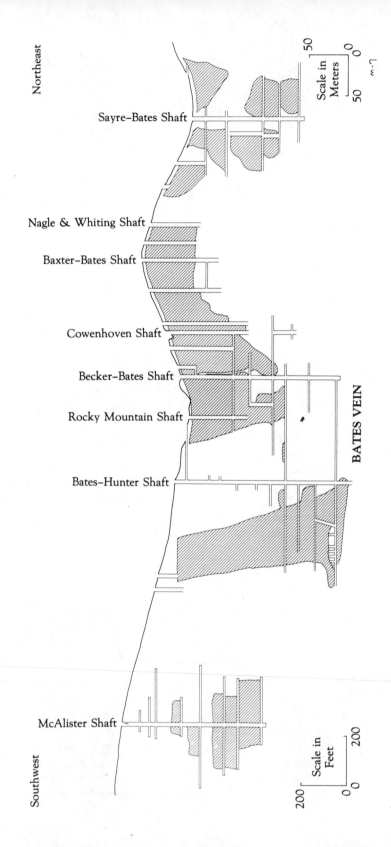

Northeast

Sayre–Bates Shaft

Nagle & Whiting Shaft

Baxter–Bates Shaft

Cowenhoven Shaft

Becker–Bates Shaft

Rocky Mountain Shaft

Bates–Hunter Shaft

McAlister Shaft

Southwest

BATES VEIN

Scale in
Meters

50

0

50

0

m.-ʒ

Scale in
Feet

200

0

200

0

Prospectors attacked the deposit and opened mines every hundred feet along the vein. Problematically, though, the vein occurred near the top of Bobtail Hill, and there was little water. Unable to sluice their dirt, prospectors sold and traded their rich claims during the first few years for next to nothing.

Since mines never operated for long, the abandoned holes gradually filled with water. Mine drainage, then, became a major problem on the Bobtail, and drainage of all the small mines demanded a major investment.

It took until 1869, two years after Hill's smelter opened, for the Consolidated Bobtail Company to finally devise a satisfactory drainage project. The company completed the Bobtail Tunnel in 1873, and it efficiently drained the vein and much of the surrounding area.

Gold production from the Bobtail picked up, and miners took out about 140,000 ounces of gold in the next six years. The trend toward property consolidation continued, and in 1885, investors created the Gregory–Bobtail Company. It added still more holdings to the Bobtail properties. Production continued for the next twenty-five years, and the large Fifty Gold Mines complex eventually bought the property in the early 1900s.

Total gold production from the vein is uncertain, but it was probably in the range of 200,000 to 250,000 ounces. The amount of silver removed was probably twice as large. Most activity on the Bobtail ceased by 1910, although there was some activity in 1934 after the price of gold jumped to $35 per ounce. The upper portions of the mine are almost entirely worked out, and the lower portions, below the tunnel level, are flooded.

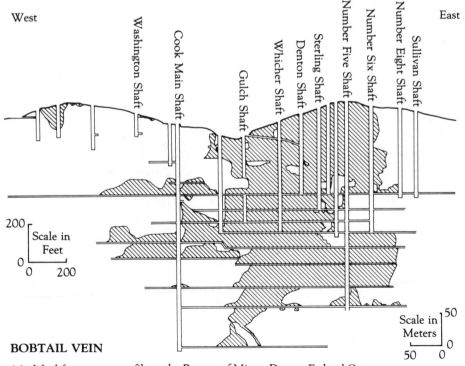

BOBTAIL VEIN

Modified from maps on file at the Bureau of Mines, Denver Federal Center.

This is the large Black Hawk mill that was located just north of the mouth of Gregory Gulch. Note the Colorado Central locomotive in the foreground and a horsedrawn wagon dumping at the mill.—*Photo by Charles Weitfle. Courtesy of the Colorado Historical Society.*

This electric locomotive served the Bobtail Tunnel. It was headed toward the Fifty Gold Mines mill at Black Hawk. Portions of the Bobtail Tunnel are still intact, and the tunnel has been used sporadically as an exhibition mine for summer visitors.—*Courtesy Western History Department, Denver Public Library.*

## Boodle Mine

You can find the Boodle Mine near the Central City cemeteries, about a mile west of town. The mine is sporadically active, so please stay away from the fenced private property. The tall structure you will see is the hoist house, and it sits over the 300–foot main shaft.

Prospectors discovered the Boodle vein sometime in the late 1880s, but early mine development was minimal. The few records that remain show that almost all the mine's gold production occurred from 1899 to 1903. The mine also produced some gold during the first and second world wars. As usual, the upper parts of the vein nearest the surface contained fair gold values, but the richness dropped off below the 100–foot level. Whether the gold values increase below the lowest level of the mine is not yet known.

All mine maps remain the confidential property of the mine owners, so none are yet available to the public. However, mine descriptions available from the Bureau of Mines in Denver allow a rough sketch of what the mine might look like.

West            Boddle Shaft            East

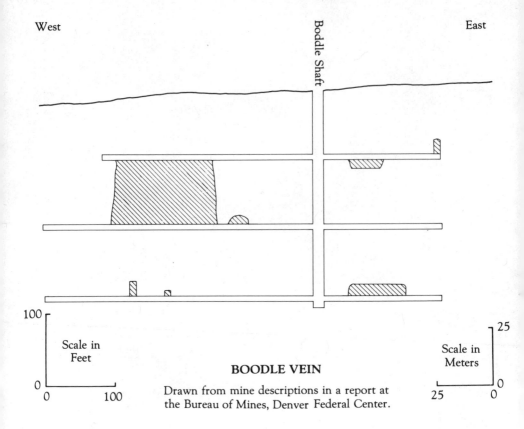

100

Scale in
Feet

0

0           100

25

Scale in
Meters

0

25        0

**BOODLE VEIN**

Drawn from mine descriptions in a report at
the Bureau of Mines, Denver Federal Center.

# Buell Mine

Surface evidence of the Buell mine is practically nonexistent today. The large hoist house is gone, but was once situated between the two one–way branches of the present–day road leading into Central City from Black Hawk. Developed to about 750 feet deep, the mine had many levels and boasted a large mill along Gregory Gulch. Total production from the mine probably exceeded 35,000 ounces of gold and 100,000 ounces of silver.

Over the years, the Buell mine operated on several splinters of a vein system that ran northeast and southwest from Gregory Gulch. There were several different names for the system, depending on where a shaft intersected the vein. Leavitt, Kip, Vasa, Wain, and U.P.R. are the most common.

Like the nearby Bates vein, most of the development took place on the central part of the vein near Gregory Gulch. There, most of the mineralization was confined to one discrete zone. Away from the gulch, however, the zone split up into smaller veins, and there were perpetual lawsuits over ownership. In fact, many mines on the Buell were in court more than they were in production.

From 1872 to 1875, the Buell mine was the county's largest producer, thanks to good equipment and good mining conditions. Certainly good planning played a part, too. Unlike many mines, the Buell collected water near

An undated photograph near the main shaft in the Buell mine hoist house. The man at the far right is R.L. Martin, the mine manager.—*Courtesy Western History Department, Denver Public Library.*

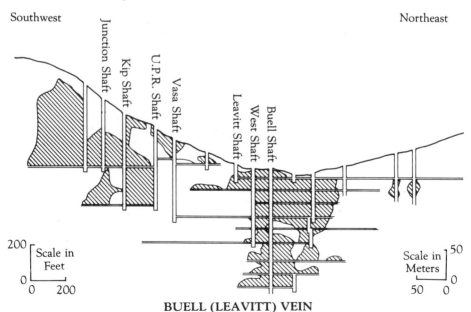

**BUELL (LEAVITT) VEIN**

Modified from maps in Bastin & Hill (1917) and unpublished maps on file at the Colorado School of Mines.

the surface before it got deep in the mine and became an expensive problem.

By the 1890s, the mine ran short of high-grade ore near the surface. Unfortunately, the property was not large enough to independently support the increased investments needed to go to greater depths. Had someone combined the Buell with adjacent properties, the mine might have stayed in production for another ten or fifteen years. By the 1900s, though, most of the mine owners had spent their profits in court. They could no longer afford to stay in business.

## Burroughs Vein

Ben Burroughs discovered the Burroughs vein on Quartz Hill south of Nevadaville during the rush of May 1859. Like others in the district, technical and financial problems idled mines on the Burroughs time and again. They never produced for more than a few years in a row. Nonetheless, the Burroughs lode produced considerable gold, and some parts produced until

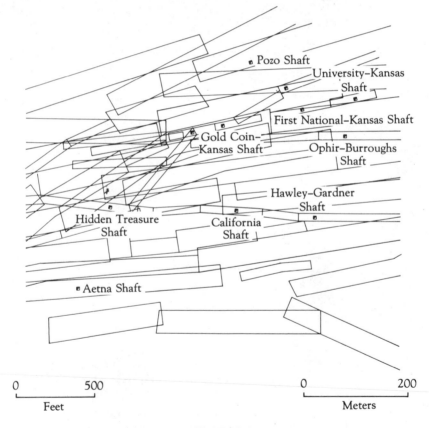

**CLAIMS**

An example of a confusing swarm of claims just south of Nevadaville. Claims followed individual veins, and where the veins were near one another, claims overlapped. The density of claims in the area shown is typical of the district. (Modified from Bastin & Hill, 1917.)

1939. Total output from all mines on the Burroughs is probably 45,000 ounces of gold and 79,000 ounces of silver.

Four mines controlled most of the vein: Mackey-Burroughs, Phoenix-Burroughs, Conley-Burroughs, and Ophir-Burroughs. During the period of greatest production, no single company ever controlled the whole length of the vein. Each operation desired secrecy, and there are no maps that show all the mining on the Burroughs.

The Ophir was the richest mine on the vein. In 1874, with its shaft at 750 feet, it was the deepest mine in Colorado. By the next year, the shaft was 915 feet deep and the press touted the mine as "one of the richest in the territory." The gold percentage decreased with depth, however, and shaft digging stopped at 1,000 feet in 1876.

The Burroughs vein extended a little over a half mile along the surface. Underground, miners found the Burroughs intersected the Kansas Vein at depth. Contrary to the normal practice of costly litigation, the owners merged the two properties in 1875. The combined Kansas-Burroughs Company went on to become one of the largest single producers in the entire region. Its total output probably exceeded $3 million (about $65 million at today's prices).

# California—Hidden Treasure—Gardner Vein

Several prospectors independently discovered different parts of this important vein in 1860. Like others found on Quartz Hill, the vein was very rich. The main sections of the vein were the Hidden Treasure on the west end, the California in the middle, and the Gardner on the east end. The vein was probably the second richest in the entire region, the Gregory being the richest. From discovery to last known production in 1938, the vein yielded about 425,000 ounces of gold and 1,400,000 ounces of silver.

Development on the deposit mirrored the typical pattern of feverish activity followed by stagnation. After Hill's smelter revived miniinig in 1867, companies rapidly deepened the main shafts in search of more ore. By the early 1870s, however, pessimistic reports proclaimed that the mines were exhausted.

The mines stayed idle until Joseph Standley bought the California mine in 1877. He was a thoughtful new investor with great plans for the mine. He studied all the old maps and records in detail before he made his first move. And his first move was daring and expensive.

First, he abandoned the old, 740-foot inclined shaft and dug a completely new, vertical shaft nearby. Only a few feet below the lowest level of the old shaft, he found rich new ore. Leaving the ore intact, he then developed several new shafts and levels. Over the next two years, he deepened the main California shaft to a record depth of 940 feet. With the mine developed in a logical manner, Standley knew exactly where to find all the good ore. He knew how much gold he had, and how much profit he would make.

Next door, the owners of the Hidden Treasure mine must have thought Standley had the right idea, because they imitated his plan practically move for move. Like Standley, they abandoned their old shaft and found new ore at the bottom of their new shaft. Both mines prospered.

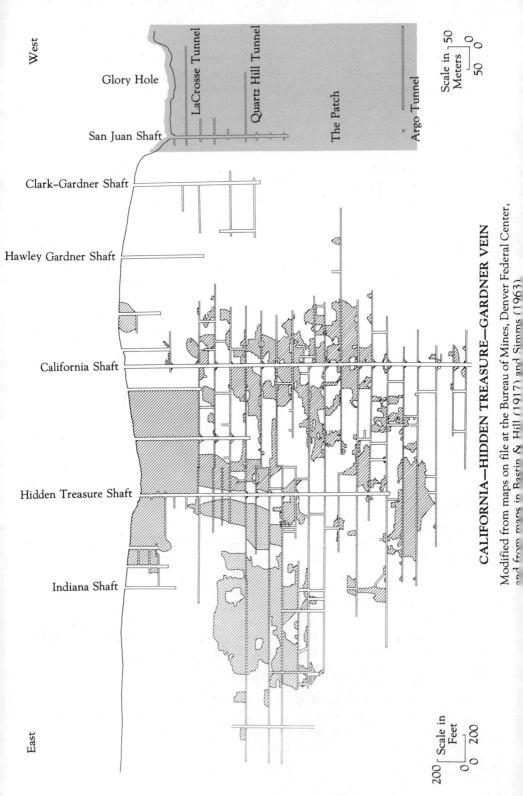

West

Glory Hole

San Juan Shaft

Clark–Gardner Shaft

Hawley Gardner Shaft

California Shaft

Hidden Treasure Shaft

Indiana Shaft

East

LaCrosse Tunnel

Quartz Hill Tunnel

The Patch

Argo Tunnel

Scale in Meters

50

0

50

0

50

Scale in Feet

200

0

200

**CALIFORNIA–HIDDEN TREASURE–GARDNER VEIN**

Modified from maps on file at the Bureau of Mines, Denver Federal Center, and from maps in Bastin & Hill (1917) and Simms (1963).

For a few years, the two mines seemed to be in a constant race to be the state's deepest mine. By 1881, the Hidden Treasure had reached 1,275 feet but was still behind the California. The race ended a couple of years later when the California bought the Hidden Treasure mine and combined the holdings into an even more profitable company.

The rare luxury of planning paid off handsomely in steady gold production for the mines throughout the 1880s. With no need for competing shafts, the company deepened the California shaft only as much as needed for future work. The California retained its status as the deepest shaft in the state and eventually bottomed out at 2,250 feet in 1892.

At a depth of almost a half mile, water became a phenomenal problem. The problem worsened when the nearby Kansas mine shut down in the early 1890s. By 1893, water had completely inundated the Kansas workings. As feared, water began leaking into the California–Hidden Treasure mine in unstoppable amounts. Soon, the company abandoned the deepest sections of the mine. By 1896, it had to abandon the whole mine.

Ten years later, the Argo Tunnel drained the California–Hidden Treasure mine, but water damage had been too severe. Sadly for the owners, they were only able to remove a small amount of gold from the mine again.

There was, however, quite a bit of gold still left in the Gardner end of the vein. Heavy water inflow was mitigated somewhat, and gold extraction continued in the Gardner mine until after World War I.

The Gilpin Tram's *Quartz Hill* locomotive at the huge California mine near Nevadaville. Dressed in a suit is Fred Kruse, the line's general manager.—*Courtesy of the Colorado Historical Society, H.H. Buckwalter Collection.*

The large Hidden Treasure mill, with its forty-foot waterwheel, is on the right side of Clear Creek, and the Gilpin Tramway is on the left. The mill is gone, but the railroad grade can still be seen at Black Hawk's northern town boundary.—*Photo by Henry H. Lake, 1899. Courtesy Western History Department, Denver Public Library.*

A stereoscopic photograph of gold sponge left after mercury was driven out of amalgam. The legend on the back reads, "This interesting pile of gold is the result of four weeks' run of the 'Hidden Treasure' Mining Company. Weight 1,370 ozs.; value $22,500." Unimpressive in black and white, this ten-inch pile would have been worth about $490,000 today.—*Photo by Charles Weitfle. Courtesy Western History Department, Denver Public Library.*

# Coeur d'Alene Mine

The hoist house of the Coeur d'Alene mine overlooked the south end of Central City for the better part of a century. Like a sentinel, it stood as a symbol of better days when gold and "the Little Kingdom of Gilpin" reigned supreme. Once slated as a museum for the Central City Opera House, the building fell into disrepair. It finally fell victim to heavy, crushing snows in the winter of 1986–1987.

The mine's location above Central City made it a prominent landmark, but the mine was never a large producer. Prospectors probably found the vein sometime in the 1870s but did little work. In 1884, new prospectors reopened an "old abandoned shaft" above Central City and christened it the Coeur d'Alene after the famous Idaho silver district. Unfortunately, the vein was never very rich nor very reliable.

The main shaft was 700 feet deep. There were six levels of workings, and none extended more than 250 feet away from the shaft. Sometime after the turn of the century, investors incorporated the property as the School Hill Mining Company. A one-page company prospectus from that era survives in the Denver Public Library.

A huge crowd around the Hubert mill near Nevadaville. The Hubert was one of scores of similar mills that once dotted the landscape all across Gilpin County. The California mine sits high on the hill beyond.—*Courtesy Western History Department, Denver Public Library.*

A sign between Central City and Nevadaville pointing the way to the Coeur d'Alene mine.—*Author's Photo.*

## Fisk—Sleepy Hollow—After Supper Vein

The Fisk, Sleepy Hollow, and After Supper lodes are names for different sections of a vein system that runs from Black Hawk to the top of Bobtail Hill. Typically, prospectors named veins as they found them and cared little if they were extensions of other known veins.

Prospectors probably discovered the heavily mineralized Fisk section first. Miners sunk a number of shallow shafts there in the 1860s, but development was slow. It was not until after the Bobtail Tunnel intersected the west end of the vein in 1873 that any serious mining took place. After the tunnel drained the vein, miners dug the large Cook shaft and full-scale mining started.

In 1906, the FIfty Gold Mines Company bought rights to the west end of the Fisk along with many other veins. The Fisk intersected several important veins, including the Great Mammoth, Puzzle, Cook, and Bobtail. With access to so many veins, the company efficiently worked several mines on several veins at once.

The Fisk vein branched toward the east, and prospectors finally found one of the offshoots in 1875. Named the Sleepy Hollow, miners worked the vein to over 1,100 feet deep. Between the Fisk and the Sleepy Hollow mines was the American mine, about which little is written. Its name eventually metamorphosed into the "Americus," and its hoist house became a prominent landmark above Black Hawk during the 1890s.

The vein continues as the After Supper vein on the east side of Clear Creek. Like other veins in the eastern part of the gold field, the After Supper section was fairly rich in silver.

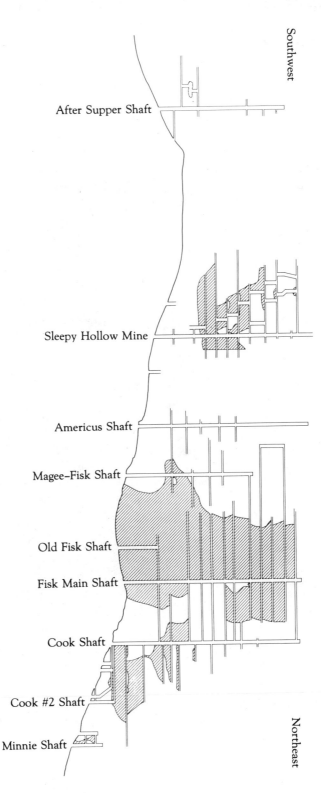

**FISK—SLEEPY HOLLOW—AFTER SUPPER VEIN**

A compilation of several maps including those on file at the Bureau of Mines, Denver Federal Center, and maps in Bastin & Hill (1917) and Simms (1963).

Southwest

After Supper Shaft

Sleepy Hollow Mine

Americus Shaft

Magee-Fisk Shaft

Old Fisk Shaft

Fisk Main Shaft

Cook Shaft

Cook #2 Shaft

Minnie Shaft

Northeast

Scale in Feet
200 0 200

Scale in Meters
50 0 50

The funeral procession for fourteen men killed by a flood in the Americus and Sleepy Hollow mines on August 29, 1895.—*Courtesy Western History Department, Denver Public Library.*

An undated photograph of Bobtail Hill near Black Hawk showing the Fisk and Nemaha mines.—*Courtesy Western History Department, Denver Public Library.*

# Gregory Vein

It's amazing to think John Gregory found not only the first vein deposit in the area, he found the very richest. Certainly luck and skill came together that fateful day of May 6, 1859.

According to Gregory, his first pan of dirt from the vein probably yielded $4 worth of gold. That works out to about a quarter ounce of gold and would be worth $87 today. That was a phenomenal amount. An early account claimed that with five people and a sluice, Gregory removed $972 worth of gold in ten days. Accounting for impurities, Gregory would have collected about 56 ounces of gold. Fifty-six ounces would be worth over $21,000 today.

In the early years, miners worked the Gregory vein intensely. Its richness was legendary. Practically every company in the region compared its property to the golden wealth of the Gregory. Contemporary companies generously sprinkled their stock offerings with phrases like "as rich as the Gregory" or "rivals the Gregory." Seldom, however, even in that period of hyperbole, was any company reckless enough to say its deposit was superior. That would have verged on heresy.

The Gregory lode, about four-tenths of a mile west of Black Hawk, was the focal point of early mining activity. Mines on the Gregory were often the first to experience problems that would later beset other operations. Being among the first to contend with troubles, however, allowed the Gregory mines to be the first to find the solutions. One of the earliest problems encountered, and solved, was the inefficient mining caused by the small, 100-foot claims.

Claim consolidation began in 1864 with the Consolidated Gregory Company, and it reached its zenith in 1906 with the Fifty Gold Mines Company. Other big names in the long history of mining on the Gregory lode were the Briggs, Narragansett, Rocky Mountain, Black Hawk, United Gregory, Consolidated Bobtail, Gregory-Bobtail, New Gregory, and Gregory-Bates.

With all these names came a lot of mining, but no one knows exactly how much. Several authors estimate production from the Gregory lode at $10 million. In round numbers, total production should work out to about 450,000 ounces of gold and 675,000 ounces of silver. At today's prices, Gregory production would be worth about $207 million.

The exact ratio of gold to silver is unknown. Miners said the upper parts of the vein contained more gold and the lowest workings showed more silver. They also said that gold values dropped from about 2.5 ounces per ton near the surface to a less than 0.5 ounces per ton at depth. Although drainage was a problem, it was probably this downward decrease in ore value that limited the mine to only about 900 feet deep. As shown on the map, though, miners removed practically every bit of usable ore down to a depth of 500 feet. Certainly little high-grade ore remains today.

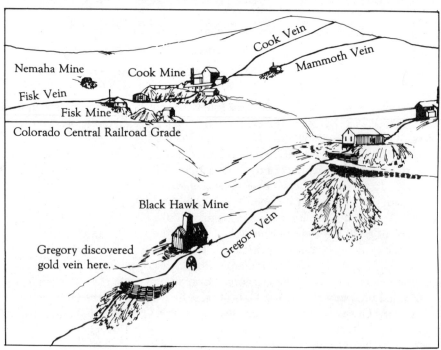

# EXPERIENCE DIDN'T ALWAYS HELP

On Sunday night, a man was found at the bottom of the Black Hawk Company's shaft at the foot of the Gregory lead. At first it was thought that something criminal was connected with the affair, but on the examination before the Coroner, it was presumed that the death was accidental as the man was seen to go into the shaft house about 8 o'clock Sunday morning and was not seen afterwards until discovered by the workman who commenced the night shift for the weeks work.

The body was severely burned and cut by the fall of 116 feet.

There were many accidents similar to this one reported in the December 30, 1862, issue of the *Central City Tri-Weekly Mining Life.* And like this case, many victims were experienced miners, not raw recruits. Apparently, novices didn't have the casual disregard for everyday danger that the seasoned miner did.

This was where John Gregory first discovered gold veins in Colorado in 1859.— *Courtesy Western History Department, Denver Public Library.*

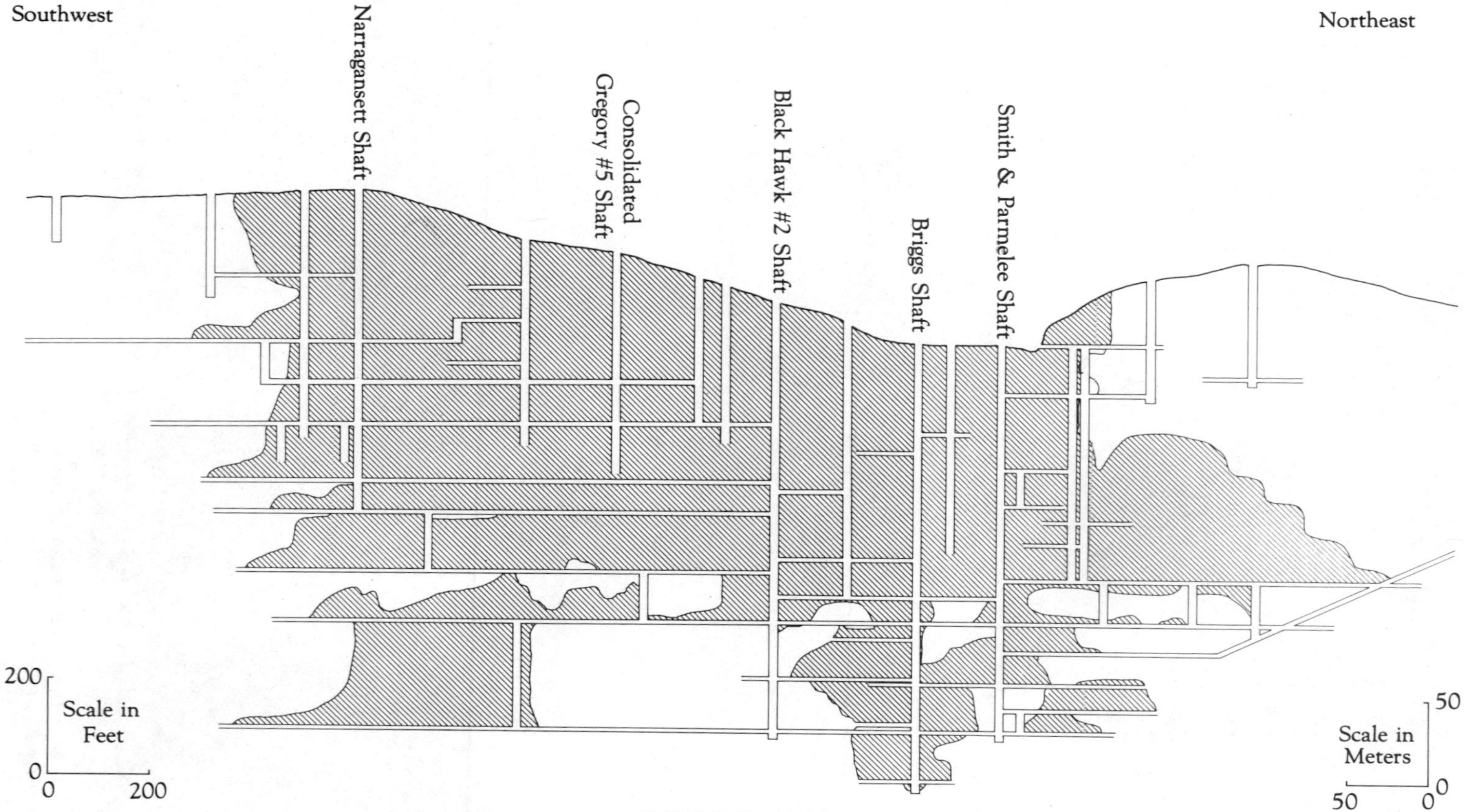

Northeast

Southwest

Smith & Parmelee Shaft

Briggs Shaft

Black Hawk #2 Shaft

Consolidated
Gregory #5 Shaft

Narragansett Shaft

GREGORY VEIN

Modified from maps on file at the Bureau of Mines, Denver Federal Center,
and the Colorado Historical Society.

Scale in
Meters

50

0

50

0

Scale in
Feet

200

0

200

# Gunnell Lode

The Gunnell, about a mile west of Central City, was another of the veins discovered in the 1859 gold rush. Miners developed several small operations during the early days, but mining really didn't get going strong until the 1870s.

By that time, richer companies had combined the small claims into three large properties: the Gunnell, the Concrete, and the Grand Army. In later years, miners on the Gunnell vein drove connections to the Argo Tunnel and the Golden Treasure mine. Total production for the whole deposit, from 1859 to 1938, was probably about 206,000 ounces of gold and 440,000 ounces of silver. While the Gunnell was certainly a large producer, it is old-fashioned intrigue that makes its story interesting.

In the mid-1870s, there were just two big operations working the vein: the combined Grand Army–Gunnell mine and the Concrete mine. The Grand

The Grand Central mine was located a short distance south of the Gunnell mine and north of Nevadaville. The dump from the mine is extensive, but few records exist to indicate how rich the mine was.—*Courtesy Western History Department, Denver Public Library.*

# TOTAL PRODUCTION

From 1859 to 1894, Gilpin County led all other Colorado counties in the production of gold. However, prospectors found huge deposits of gold near Cripple Creek in 1891, and that district soon overshadowed Central City and Gilpin County. Nonetheless, Gilpin County still ranks as the second most productive county in the state. (Teller County, which included the Cripple Creek district, recovered four times as much gold.)

Silver was never the economic mainstay of Central City that it was of Leadville, Aspen, Creede, and Georgetown. Still, as a by–product of gold smelting, total production topped $9 million. Copper, lead, and zinc extraction added another $6.3 million.

The numbers are factual, but they're misleading. The value of the U.S. dollar and the price of metals are always fluctuating. Besides, with the huge dollar values we hear every day on the news, we have the tendency to ask, "So what?"

The answer is that the U.S. dollar used to be worth more in the past. To get a better picture, let's first find out how much metal the old miners removed. Then, if we calculate out how much that metal would be worth today, we see much more impressive value:

| COMMODITY | WEIGHT | VALUE (1988) |
|---|---|---|
| Gold | 4,248,608 ounces | $1,911,873,600 |
| Silver | 11,044,000 ounces | 82,830,000 |
| Copper | 25,500,000 pounds | 22,860,000 |
| Lead | 35,400,000 pounds | 14,826,000 |
| Zinc | 330,000 pounds | 141,800 |
|  |  | $2,032,531,400 |

## GILPIN COUNTY VALUE OF METALS PRODUCED
### 1859 TO PRESENT TOTAL VALUE $105,125,032

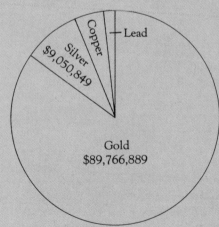

Copper

Silver $9,050,849

— Lead

Gold
$89,766,889

80

Army was the deepest. When its shaft reached 700 feet in 1874, its miners discovered a rich pocket of ore. From the descriptions of talkative miners, the owners of the Concrete mine reasoned the new ore body would extend under their land,too.

They started digging a new shaft to intersect the discovery on their land. What they didn't know was that Grand Army miners had already trespassed and stolen thousands of tons of rich ore that rightfully belonged to the Concrete mine.

As the new Concrete shaft neared the illegal workings, Grand Army workers tried to sabotage further advance. They burned foul-smelling sulfur bombs. They set off dynamite charges. Gold was involved, though, and the Concrete mine owners weren't deterred by the high jinks.

Nor were they happy with the theft. When the new shaft hit mine voids where the ore should have been, the Concrete mine owners were furious. They sought revenge and retribution in court. And they won. In fact, the court awarded them all rights to the remaining ore on the Grand Army-Gunnell property.

The combined mines proved quite profitable until a disastrous pump house fire in 1904. With the pumps destroyed, the mine couldn't hold back the unending water seepage, and most of the mine flooded out. Eventually, the Tremont Company, a subsidiary of the Argo Tunnel, purchased the property and worked it intermittently until about 1938.

# Kansas Vein

The surface expression of the Kansas vein lies only a couple of hundred feet south of the dirt road to Nevadaville. Several principle mines shared the lode: Alger, English, University, First National, Monmouth, and Gold Coin. Together the mines produced an estimated 190,000 ounces of gold and 690,000 ounces of silver. There were underground connections to the California-Hidden Treasure vein and the Burroughs vein.

Most maps to the various mines are apparently still secret today. The only publicly available map is that of the Gold Coin, and it shows considerable mining between the 500- and 1,000-foot levels. Its 1,350-foot Gold Coin shaft was the deepest on the deposit. Reports say the other mines worked extensively down to 500 feet or so.

The Kansas mines are so close to a popular road that they pose special hazards for people looking for souvenirs or spots to photograph. The land is privately owned, and any shallow depression could be a loosely covered deep shaft.

Records show high gold values deep in the Kansas vein, but water was too great a problem for the mines. The vein was finally abandoned and allowed to flood in the late 1880s, and it remained that way for almost fifty years. However, with the jump in the price of gold to $35 an ounce in 1934, miners reexamined the Kansas vein with new interest.

They hoped to drain the flooded Kansas mines through the Argo Tunnel, and numerous attempts were made to locate the bottom of the old workings. Fully knowledgeable of the tremendous volume of water that lay overhead, miners drove adits and raises for almost a decade before they finally found the rich Kansas vein late in 1942. Even though they proceeded cautiously in horribly treacherous conditions, an unknown amount of rock finally gave way during blasting on Saturday, January 19, 1943. The resulting flood killed four men and washed so much rock and debris into the tunnel that no one ever attempted mining on the Kansas vein again.

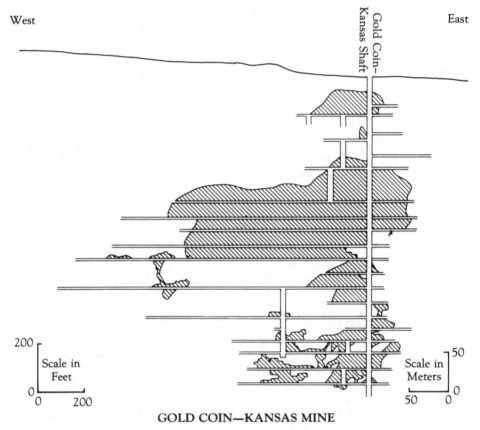

**GOLD COIN—KANSAS MINE**

Modified from a map in a prospectus for the Gold Coin Mines Co., Western History Department, Denver Public Library.

# Old Town Vein

Most of the mines around Russell Gulch were smaller than the ones around Central City; the largest was the Old Town. Unlike most of the veins, the Old Town was a lot richer at depth than it was near the surface. That is probably why no one developed the mine until the 1880s or 1890s. Even then, workers from another mine, not the Old Town, actually found the richest part of the deposit. Miners were working the Wautauga vein and found that it intersected the Old Town vein at depth. A short–lived litigation over ownership of the combined vein followed. The two companies merged in 1902 and settled the case.

While most other producing mines were in middle and old ages by that time, the Old Town mine was an energetic newcomer. Moreover, it benefited from forty years of mining experience around Central City. Consequently, it showed fairly steady gold production for almost all of the next forty–two years. By 1944, when it finally closed, the Old Town shaft was 1,400 feet deep, and miners had extracted some 132,000 ounces of gold and 346,000 ounces of silver. The mine was partially rehabilitated during the 1950s search for uranium, but there was never any significant new production.

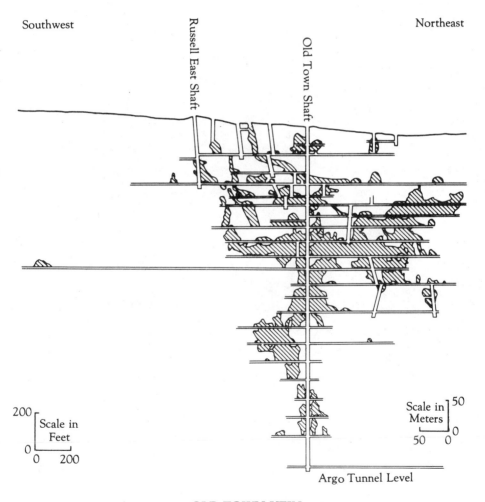

**OLD TOWN VEIN**

Modified from maps in Sims (1963) and Bastin & Hill (1917).

# The Patch, or Glory Hole

In two isolated instances around Central City, gold occurred in situations other than vein deposits. The largest of these was the Patch on Quartz Hill south of Nevadaville. The Patch was a chimney–shaped deposit of broken, crushed rock that geologists termed a stockwork. Instead of finding gold concentrated in veins as they did elsewhere, miners found gold spread throughout the whole broken mass of the Patch.

Miners first encountered the Patch while working the San Juan mine in 1874 and their discovery proved problematical. Elsewhere, they were used to mining discrete veins. If the vein had gold, they knew they could follow it. In the Patch, though, they didn't find veins. They found gold concentrated in tiny veinlets, as well as in the wall rock itself. Often miners couldn't tell where the ore stopped and the wall rock began. They couldn't figure out an efficient way to extract all the ore.

Looking west toward Nevadaville, we see the Chain O'Mines mill and its tailings ponds. In the foreground is the partially drowned Colorado & Southern depot, now deep under the parking lot at the south end of Central City.—*Courtesy Western History Department, Denver Public Library.*

Production from the Patch puttered along. Miners selectively removed only the richest parts of the deposit and left the rest. Unfortunately, burrowing through the deposit in small, twisting tunnels was inefficient. They had to stop and analyze the rock every few feet to find out where the gold was. Finally, ventilation, water, and financial problems closed the San Juan mine in 1893. It was reopened in 1906 and worked sporadically by a succession of different owners until 1915.

Overlapping claims across the deposit were a nightmare. William Muchow finally came along in 1927 and figured out how to mine the Patch. Like other successful property owners across the district, he first combined all the claims under one ownership. His development scheme was the picture of simplicity: mine and mill everything.

He renovated the old LaCrosse and Quartz Hill tunnels that cut through the Patch at levels of 235 and 1,583 feet below the surface. Using them to remove ore, he developed a large cave by blasting overlying rock down into the tunnels. Through controlled blasting, he brought the roof down and gradually created a large hole on the surface. The "Glory Hole" progressively grew to about 400 feet across. Because of the strange method of mining, the Glory Hole attracted a lot of visitors and became quite a tourist attraction during the 1930s.

Muchow's Chain O'Mines mill at Central City was huge. Since it processed everything mined from the Glory Hole, it discarded staggering tonnages of

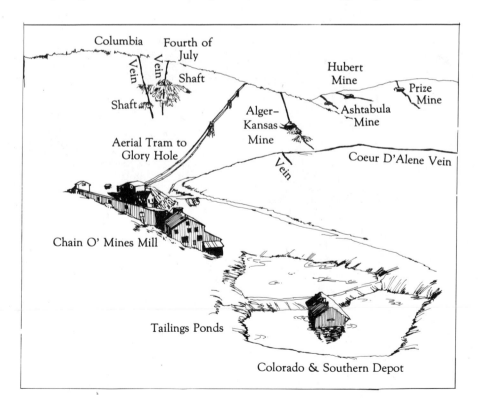

85

A 1977 view of the LaCrosse Tunnel deep beneath the Glory Hole.—*Author's Photo.*

Other mills paled in comparison with the sheer size of the Chain O'Mines mill at the south end of Central City. The old Colorado & Southern depot can be seen a few hundred feet down the valley from the lowest part of the mill.—*Photo from the* Mining Review, *Salt Lake City. Courtesy Western History Department, Denver Public Library.*

useless, powdered rock. The only place to dump all the waste was over Central City's old Colorado & Southern railroad depot. That depot is now buried under the yellowish rock pile that serves as the city's parking lot on the south side of town.

The Chain O'Mines operation recovered a lot of gold, but extraction costs were high. Operations tapered off in the late 1930s, and there was only minimal production during the 1940s. Water users down on the plains sued the company, claiming the mill polluted water in Clear Creek. As a settlement, the company moved its mill out of Central City in the 1940s. (It now sits along the road between Central City and Idaho Springs.)

At one time, the owners proposed a grandiose scheme to reprocess the old tailings pile, uncover the railroad depot, and turn it into a museum. Civic pride, however, couldn't replace nonexistent company profits, and the idea was forgotten.

Since that time, there has been sporadic activity around the Glory Hole every few years as the price of gold fluctuates. Although once a tourist attraction, the Glory Hole is now private property and is presently closed to the public. Moreover, it is impossible to find visible gold in the Glory Hole. Looking there will prove both fruitless and very dangerous. Please stay out.

## Prize Vein

Running along the hill immediately to the north of Nevadaville are the Prize and Seuderberg veins. The two are separate, parallel veins near the surface, but they converge to form one rich vein at depth. Two independent and profitable companies worked the veins separately until the 1870s when they discovered the veins intersected. As usual, each company sued the other, claiming that it owned the downward continuation of the united vein. For eight years, only the companies' lawyers made any money.

Unfortunately for the lawyers, the Prize Consolidated Company settled the litigation. The company bought both properties and returned to the business of mining. From then on, production was sporadic because of water problems. However, the ore was rich and the mine ranked among the top producers in the area. Records suggest the mine produced about 130,000 ounces of gold and 310,000 ounces of silver.

The owners planned the mine's development fairly well, and it should have produced gold for many years. Mining ground to a halt, however, with the 1929 stock crash. Except for an isolated production report of seven ounces ten years later, it never reopened. Ignoring the extreme cost of extraction today, the Prize mine is possibly one of the few that still has much gold ore left.

## Saratoga Vein

Prospectors discovered the Saratoga vein east of Russell Gulch sometime before 1880. Until its closure in 1946, the Saratoga vein yielded 141,000 ounces of gold and 346,000 ounces of silver. The vein was a major producer, but it wasn't particularly rich. Its owners were just persistent.

As the mine map shows, miners worked the deposit through four shafts, and

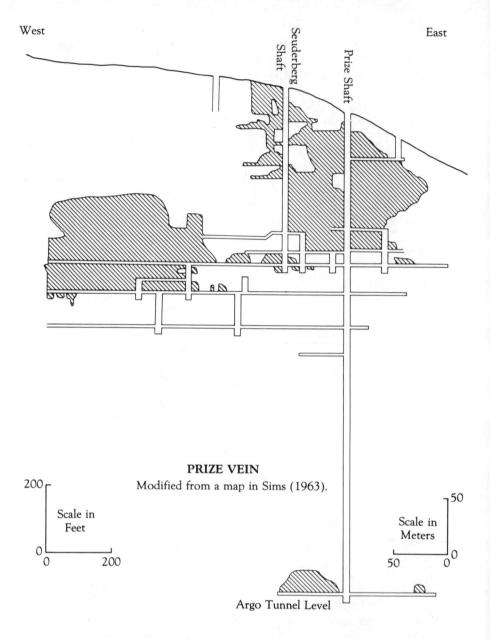

West

East

Seuderberg Shaft

Prize Shaft

**PRIZE VEIN**
Modified from a map in Sims (1963).

200

Scale in
Feet

0

0                    200

50

Scale in
Meters

50            0

0

Argo Tunnel Level

they extracted most of the vein in between. At its furthest advance, the mine was 1,200 feet deep and extended down to the level of the Argo Tunnel. Typically, the Saratoga was most lucrative in its upper 1,000 feet.

## Placer Mines

Summer visitors always notice recreational prospectors diligently panning, sluicing, and dredging alongside Highways 6 and 119 below Black Hawk. Many of them try it for themselves, at least once. Even after 130 years, many

West

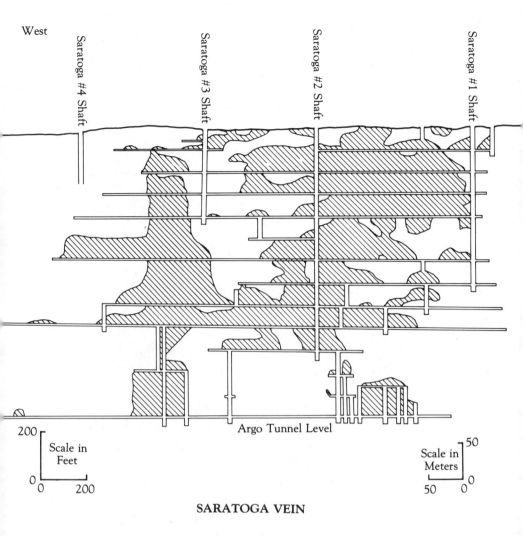

Saratoga #4 Shaft

Saratoga #3 Shaft

Saratoga #2 Shaft

Saratoga #1 Shaft

Argo Tunnel Level

200
Scale in
Feet
0
0        200

50
Scale in
Meters
0
50      0

**SARATOGA VEIN**

still find small flakes of gold every summer. What most don't know is how much mining has preceded them.

Referring to the section of Clear Creek below Black Hawk, George Crofutt concluded in 1885:

> Nearly every foot of the creek has been dug over, time and again, by miners, in search of the yellow metal, gold. Dams, in many places, have turned the waters of the creek, through flumes, first on one side of its bed, then on the other, and the greater portion of the earth, from surface to bedrock, from one side of the gulch to the other, has been dug and washed over. (From volume 2 of *Crofutt's Grip-Sack Guide of Colorado.*)

Initially, prospectors divided the creek into 100–foot–long claims, all the way from the forks of the creek to well north of Black Hawk. They claimed all the tributary drainages, like Russell Gulch, Nevada Gulch, and Gregory Gulch, in the same manner, and they even claimed some of the small gullies

89

In this 1889 shot in the Saratoga mine, we see one miner breaking ore off the right-hand wall. The other miner may be filling his box with particularly rich gold specimens.— *Courtesy Western History Department. Denver Public Library.*

coming off the hillsides. Loose companies of miners often banded together and worked several adjacent claims at once.

In the early days, there were no major corporations involved with placer mining. There was really no room for corporate investment. Compared to the lodes, placers were too small. Even with reworking, placers accounted for only about one percent of the gold extracted from the Central City and surrounding districts.

But one percent of the Central City area was not paltry. In fact, all placer mining probably netted 55,000 ounces of gold. Of that total, miners probably

This miner is shoveling ore into a cart from a chute fed by workings overhead. From the Saratoga mine, 1889.—*Courtesy Western History Department, Denver Public Library.*

extracted about 15,000 to 20,000 ounces between 1859 and 1863, all by hand.

Placer mining weakened before the Civil War, although occasional claims were reworked several times throughout the 1870s. By the 1880s, frugal Chinese miners moved in and reworked ground already considered mined-out. The Chinese were emphatically unwelcome in underground mines, but even their prejudiced opponents grudgingly respected them as excellent placer miners: "The placer mines of Gilpin County are gradually passing into the hands of the 'heathen Chinese', who make money where the Anglo-Saxon race would starve to death." (From the *Central City Weekly Register-Call*, January 7, 1881.)

Hydraulic mining, the blasting of placer gravels with thunderous water cannons, never achieved the popularity in Colorado that it had enjoyed in California during the 1850s and 1860s. One company tried it for a short while on the lower part of Clear Creek west of Golden. Public sentiment, however, loudly opposed the pollution and destruction it caused. Realistically, though, the placers on Clear Creek were probably too small for hydraulic mining.

Even the Chinese couldn't find much placer gold after the 1880s. Miners rightly concluded that if there were any gold left, it was too deep to retrieve at a profit. In 1934, though, the base price of gold jumped from $20.67 to $35 per ounce. Almost overnight, the rules of economics changed, and the Humphrey's Gold Corporation was ready to try modern earth-moving equipment.

Having started with a small floating dredge in 1932, Humphrey's had to switch to dry-land equipment because of heavy boulders. By 1934, the higher price of gold allowed the company to bring in draglines, bulldozers and a steam shovel to move large quantities of unmined gravel. By diverting the creek with heavy equipment, Humphrey's dug all the way to bedrock, where gold concentrations were the highest.

The operation was very efficient. By late 1936, it had mined all the available gravel in the main branch of Clear Creek and about two miles up the North Fork. Out of land to mine, Humphrey's dismantled its equipment at the end of the year. A couple of other companies, however, owned land further upstream and successfully continued Humphrey's methods. Between 1934 and 1941, Humphrey's and its successors removed 32,000 ounces of gold from areas considered by all to have "played out."

How much gold remains along Clear Creek and Russell Gulch today? No one knows. Undoubtedly, weekend prospectors will continue reworking the ground for decades. With equal certainty, though, each new generation will find it progressively harder to find enough gold to pay for its equipment.

To see what the old mines were really like, invest in safe, commercial mine tours. While not as thrilling as getting lost or injured on your own, you'll enjoy the adventure. And live to tell about it.—*Author's Photo*

The miners at the face are single jacking. The man with the dog and the carbide lamp was possibly a shift boss. In this shot, we see the iron sheet miners laid down at the face just before blasting. The sheet caught rocks thrown out by the blast and made shoveling easier.—*Photo by Lachlan McLean. Courtesy Western History Collections, University of Colorado.*

# MINING METHODS

The concept of digging through rock is a simple process: (1) drill small holes; (2) load them with dynamite; (3) blast the dynamite; (4) remove the broken rock; (5) repeat the process. The actual implementation though, is both the art and the science of mining, developed over centuries of sweat by common men.

## Digging Tunnels and Ore

Miners dug most of the rock from the mountains around Central City by hand. Until the introduction of mechanical steam and air drills around 1879, and for long afterward, miners drilled blast holes with hammers and drill steel. Single jacking with a four–pound sledge was the most popular method of drilling and the one shown in most old underground photographs. If a vein was wide, or a tunnel was large enough, miners switched to double jacking—one man held the steel, another swung an eight–pound hammer.

Miner drilled holes in widely variable patterns, depending on the hardness of the rock and the width of the vein. In general, though, they drilled three holes at various angles near the center of the working face. The miners wanted these holes to almost intersect a few feet into the rock. Around the edges of the face, they drilled more holes in the direction they wanted the passage to go. Next they loaded the holes with dynamite. (They used rolls of black powder before 1868.) After attaching precise lengths of fuse to the charges, they headed for the surface.

In small mines one miner was responsible for lighting all the fuses. As the other miners headed out of the mine, he stayed behind to light the fuses. After making sure all were burning properly, he retreated a safe distance down a passage and listened to the blasts go off in sequence. By counting the sounds of the blasts, he warned the next shift of potential problems. Even with such precautions, drillers occasionally found unexploded charges of dynamite with their steel. If the dynamite blew up under him, it commonly injured or killed the driller.

As a rule, miners "shot" the face near the end of their ten–hour shift. They blasted then because it took a couple of hours for the smoke and dust to clear. Moreover, fumes from exploded nitroglycerin in the dynamite caused ferocious headaches. Miners from the next shift returned, "mucked out" the broken rock, and repeated the process. Each shift normally advanced the tunnel three to six feet.

Miners cut the fuses at different lengths so they could blast the dynamite at intervals. They wanted the dynamite in the "cut" holes at the center of the face to shoot first and make a small, cone–shaped crater. Next, they wanted to fire the "reliever" holes so the dynamite would blast rock toward the newly formed cavity. The "edger" holes exploded next, followed lastly by the "lifter" holes at floor level. Really good blasters prided themselves on this last charge. They wanted the lifter shot to throw rock up and away from the face onto a piece of boilerplate to make shoveling easier. Electric blasting was introduced in the early 1870s, and it made the timing of blasts a lot easier. And safer. Unfortunately, it never completely eliminated the problem of unshot sticks of dynamite.

Miners usually developed horizontal adits, or entries, on different levels, usually a hundred feet apart. When finished, they would try to dig out all the

Double jacking. The miner on the right would have moved his arms out of the way before the man with the eight-pound sledge swung upward.—*Photo by Lachlan McLean. Courtesy Western History Collections, University of Colorado.*

# SEQUENCE OF BLASTING

1.

The blaster cuts the fuses to different lengths so the dynamite will explode at intervals. Once the fuses are lit, he heads for safety.

2.

The cut holes explode first and make a crater in the center of the face. Next, the reliever holes detonate.

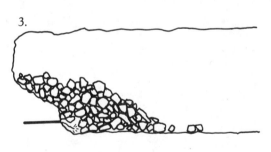

3.

Edger holes along the roof and edge of the face go off next.

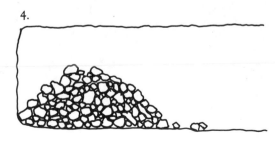

4.

Last to explode are the lifter holes. Miners return on the next shift to muck out the shattered rock.

ore in between. Miners referred to the huge narrow caverns that resulted as stopes.

Overhand stoping was the easiest way to remove ore. Miners would drill and blast rock from overhead down into the horizontal passages. As the stope got higher and higher, they wedged timbers between the walls and stood on them while they drilled. Underhand stoping was the opposite technique, and in those cases, they would drill into the floor and gradually dig out the vein under their feet.

On rather precarious footing, this miner is working in an overhand stope in the Saratoga mine, 1889.—*Courtesy Western History Department, Denver Public Library.*

# Shafts

Shaft drillers dug shafts with techniques similar to tunnelling. Mucking out the broken rock, though, was immensely harder. Shaft drilling, with the constant threat of falling rocks, was wet, dangerous business. Consequently, drillers experienced in the trade earned more than the typical underground

Looking down, we see two miners sinking a shaft. Another rare photo by Lachlan McLean.—*Courtesy Western History Collections, University of Colorado.*

miner. Shafts around Central City angled downward along the veins, and as the veins bent, so did the shafts.

Small mines normally used large buckets to haul ore, men, and water out of the shafts. Since most shafts were tilted, the buckets banged and crashed back and forth between the walls as the hoist dragged them to the surface. Occasionally, they caught on obstructions. (Many Cornish miners refused to ride in buckets, preferring instead to climb long ladders in and out of the mines.)

Here is a 1902 example of two men stuffed into an ore bucket for the ride down to workings in the Delmonico mine. Hanging onto the cable are two more miners, and the operator is sitting on a box at the left.—*Photo by A.E. Dickerson. Courtesy Western History Department, Denver Public Library.*

This cage in the Saratoga mine had rails on the floor so ore carts could be lifted to the surface. Standing are mine manager George Barret and mining engineer F.W. Englich. (1889)—*Courtesy Western History Department, Denver Public Library.*

# THE BLACK HAWK #2 SHAFT

I have very vivid recollections of being taken down this shaft where a new manila rope had recently been installed. All went well going down, but on returning to the surface the twist in the rope turned the bucket round and round. The sensation as we neared the surface was that I was upside down. We were all so dizzy that we had to be lifted from the bucket.

In a fascinating address to the State Historical Society, C.H. Hanington told stories of his 1870s childhood around Central City. This was one of his recollections of a trip down the Black Hawk #2 shaft on the Gregory lode. Remember, miners went through this routine every day. (See his address in *Colorado Magazine*, vol. 19, #1, January 1942.)

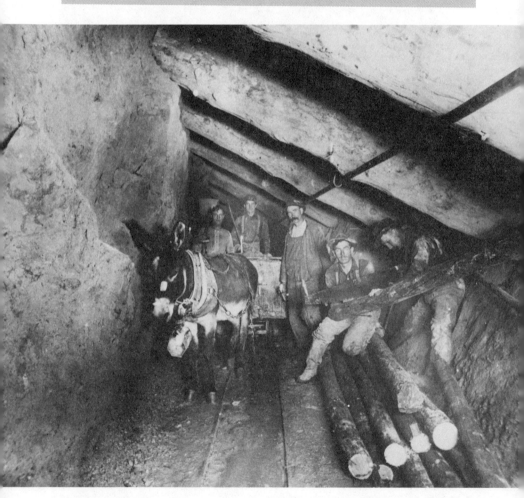

The huge timbers supporting the roof suggest this must have been a mine haulageway out of this unidentified mine.—*Photo by Lachlan McLean. Courtesy Western History Collections, University of Colorado.*

Larger mines often replaced their buckets with skips. Skips were normally iron or wooden boxes that skidded upward along wooden planks. They worked well in shafts that were more severely tilted away from vertical. A few of the most lucrative mines sunk vertical shafts off to the side of the vein so they could use cages. Essentially primitive elevators, cages were faster and much less risky than the ore buckets they replaced.

## Ore Transport

For several decades, buckets were the standard method for getting ore, men, and supplies up shafts. Getting ore from the working face to the shaft was a different problem.

In the early days before consolidation of the small mines, wheelbarrows sufficed. As the distance to the shaft increased, though, miners turned to ore cars and lightweight rails. If the mine was small and the passages were fairly flat, men would push the cars themselves. For longer distances and more ore, they

Miners at an unknown mine near Central City, probably before 1900. Note the hard, slow-burning candles they used for light.—*Courtesy Western History Department, Denver Public Library.*

laid heavier rails and brought in mules and bigger ore cars. Large operations like the Argo Tunnel and the Fifty Gold Mines Corporation used heavy electric locomotives to pull long trains of ore cars.

## Lighting

Carbide lamps were invented around 1910. Until then, three long–burning candles were the only source of light the miners had for their whole ten–hour shift. Since miners usually worked in pairs, a couple of candles gave off enough light to work by. (The candles also heated the miners' meals.) As a rule, miners stayed away from kerosene lanterns because they were both dangerous and smelly. Look carefully at most underground photographs in this book and you'll see candles stuck in the miners' felt hats or in the walls nearby.

Electric locomotive and empty ore cars at the mouth of the Argo Tunnel at Idaho Springs. The concrete portal of the tunnel is still intact and can be seen just west of the Argo Mill.—*Courtesy Western History Department, Denver Public Library.*

# IS THERE ANY GOLD LEFT?

Yes, there still is gold around Central City. Most miners know there's a lot of lower-grade ore left in mines that have been closed for decades. Moreover, practically every one of them knows of high-grade material left in old mines that closed prematurely. The problem, though, is not whether they can find gold, but whether they can mine it profitably.

More than ever before, economic reality is at odds with the gold mining mystique. Today's gold miners face tremendous economic battles that few can ever hope to win. Their labor and machinery costs are high. They now need mining and environmental permits where none were required before. They don't have any mills nearby to concentrate their ore. And even if they did, their nearest gold smelter is in El Paso, Texas. Perhaps their worst problem today is the staggering competition from huge mines in Australia, South Africa, the Soviet Union, and Canada. Because of such over-supply, some experts even predict that the price of gold will gradually fall below its current levels.

Yes, there still is gold left around Central City, but only selected mines will be able to mine it profitably.

# APPENDIX:
# CHRONOLOGY OF MINING AND RELATED DEVELOPMENTS

1859, May 6—John H. Gregory and party of Indiana prospectors discover the first gold-bearing vein deposit in the mountains.

1859, late May—Prospectors find numerous gold veins including the Bates, Bobtail, Gunnell, Gregory Extension, Gregory #2, Kansas, Burroughs.

1859, July—First water-powered mill starts work.

1860—Consolidated Ditch brings water from Fall River; miners experience first problems in separating gold from ores.

1861—Colorado Territory organized; Burdsall builds first smelter at Nevadaville, but it burns down; some mines close because of difficulty in recovering gold; back east, shooting starts in the Civil War.

1862—Investors and speculators organize numerous companies in the East to mine in Colorado; last mention of John Gregory around Central City; miners widely recognize problems with sulfides.

1863—Numerous mines close because of inability to retrieve gold from ores; most placers exhausted.

1864—Collapse of Colorado mining stocks on the eastern exchanges; feverish search for effective process to recover gold from difficult ores.

1866—James Lyon unsuccessfully tests smelter at Black Hawk.

1867—Nathaniel Hill successfully tests new Boston & Colorado smelter at Black Hawk.

1868—Boston & Colorado smelter begins commercial operation and mining starts to recover all over the district; dynamite introduced.

1870—Colorado & Southern standard-gauge railroad reaches Golden.

1872—Colorado Central narrow-gauge railroad reaches Black Hawk.

1873—Financial panic affects companies nationwide; gold production in the district slackens; Denver Smelting Company plant built at Denver; Boston & Colorado smelter at Black Hawk enlarged for refining.

# CAN YOU LEARN TO
# PAN FOR GOLD?

Sure. It's not particularly hard. If you'd like to have someone teach you, stop at one of the roadside businesses during the summer. They'll personally show you how to pan. Some will even guarantee you'll find something, and most will let you keep what you find.

If you'd rather teach yourself, you'll first have to buy a gold pan. There are two basic types: steel and plastic. They come in several sizes, but the twelve– to fourteen–inch–diameter pans are the easiest to use.

Prepare your pans before you use them. Most pans have a light coating of oil, and oil will make gold float. If you have a plastic pan, wash it with detergent. Manufacturers protect the steel pans with heavy grease, so most experienced prospectors burn the grease out in a campfire.

Next find a spot along Clear Creek where you can reach fairly calm water. It takes a lot of experience to find the best spot to pan. However, you can still find gold in Clear Creek all the way from Black Hawk to Denver. A good place to start is where other people are panning. Assume that experienced prospectors are probably working the best spots. Ask if you can watch them. Then go off by yourself and imitate their techniques.

Fill your pan with sand and gravel and cover the rocks with water. Keeping your pan tilted, and partly in the water, gradually swirl the pan around. As you wash the clay and sand over the edges, pick out the big rocks with your fingers. Try not to pan too quickly. You're trying to keep gold in the bottom of your pan while you're washing the light material over the edges.

Your first attempt will take ten or fifteen minutes, and your back will hurt by the time you finish. However, when you've washed out all the light brown material, you'll have a concentrate of black sand left in the bottom. You can either pan it down further or you can remove about half the black sand with a magnet. Now look at your pan. Closely. Do you see any yellow flakes? Those are gold!

You've heard about fool's gold. That's a mineral called pyrite. It's so much lighter than gold that most of it should have washed out of your pan. You can recognize fool's gold because it's a brassy color and water moves it easily. It only barely resembles gold, and once you've seen gold, you won't get the two confused.

Panning is hard work. After trying it, you'll realize why it was used primarily for prospecting. It was seldom used for production. Even in good placers, a day's wages in gold usually equaled about fifty pans. As a livelihood, panning just wasn't worth it.

1876—Colorado becomes thirty-eighth state.

1878—Silver veins discovered north of Black Hawk; Boston & Colorado smelter moves to Denver; Colorado Central extends railroad to Central City.

1882—Grant smelter built at Denver.

1886—Construction begins on the Gilpin Tramway; Globe smelter built at Denver.

1893—Tramway reaches most major mines in region; Silver Crash depresses the price of silver; construction begins at Argo (Newhouse) Tunnel at Idaho Springs.

1895—Accidental connection with old water-filled mines kills fourteen miners in the Americus and Sleepy Hollow mines near Black Hawk.

1897—Water successfully added to air drill for dust control.

1899—American Smelting and Refining Company (ASARCO) organized; Colorado & Southern Railroad acquires Colorado Central.

1906—Colorado & Southern Railroad purchases the Gilpin Tramway and renames it the Gilpin Railroad.

1908—Gold production from Gilpin County begins steady decrease.

1909—Fire destroys part of the Boston & Colorado smelter.

1910—Argo Tunnel completed, 4.16 miles long; Boston & Colorado smelter closes permanently.

1913—Argo Mill built at the mouth of the Argo Tunnel.

1917—Gilpin Railroad discontinues service.

1925—Colorado & Southern discontinues service to Central City.

1934—Government raises price of gold to $35 per ounce; modern placer operations start on Clear Creek.

1941—Colorado & Southern discontinues rail service to Black Hawk.

1943—Miners accidently dig into old water-filled part of the Kansas mine, and resulting flood closes Argo Tunnel.

1953—Some uranium mined west and south of. Central City.

1968—United States off gold standard, price of gold allowed to float with world demand; new interest in mining proves short-lived.

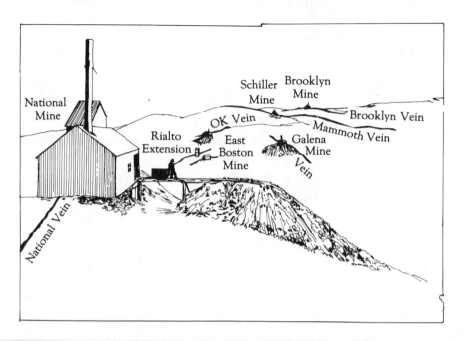

Looking toward Central City and Mammoth Hill from the tailings of the National mine. Date uncertain, but probably 1910–1915.—*Courtesy Western History Department, Denver Public Library.*

# GLOSSARY

AMALGAMATION. The process by which mercury is alloyed with gold, silver, copper, or other metals. If you've ever played with mercury and stuck it to a ring or a coin, you've seen amalgamation.

CLAIM. A parcel of public land that a person is legally entitled to mine.

LODE. A valuable mineral deposit found in the earth's surface; generally synonymous with VEIN.

MILL. A industrial plant where ore is concentrated and/or valuable metals recovered.

ORE. The commercially profitable portion of a mineral deposit; around Central City, most ores were made up of sulfur compounds that contained significant quantities of gold, silver, copper, lead, and zinc.

PAN. A circular pan with sloping sides used for finding gold, generally ten to sixteen inches in diameter and two to three inches deep, made out of steel, copper, or plastic.

PLACER. A deposit of sand and gravel containing valuable quanties of gold, silver, and other minerals.

SHAFT. A vertical, or nearly vertical, hole dug in the ground. Roughly analogous to an elevator shaft, a mine shaft may extend from the surface downward or between different levels of a mine; around Central City, most mine shafts followed gold veins and were inclined as much as twenty degrees from vertical. The deepest shaft in the area was 2,250 feet deep.

SLUICE. A long, trough–like box through which placer gravel is washed by a stream of water; gold particles are caught in the bottom by a variety of wooden bars, metal bars, rocks, cloth, or carpet.

SMELT. To melt ore in a furnace in order to separate valuable metals from worthless rock.

VEIN. A clearly defined zone of mineralized rock generally having a more or less regular development in length, width, and depth.

# SUGGESTED READINGS
# AND
# ADDITIONAL INFORMATION

There are a number of general works dealing with the history of Colorado, but my favorite is Carl Ubbelohde's very readable *A Colorado History* (6th edition, 1988). Tending toward the ponderous are the multivolume classics including Frank Hall's four-volume *History of the State of Colorado* (1889-1895) and Wilbur Stone's *History of Colorado* (4 vols., 1918-1919).

If you would like to focus on the local history of Central City, Black Hawk, and Gilpin County, a good place to start is Caroline Bancroft's 1958 narrative work, *Gulch of Gold*. You might also like to look up *Colorado's Little Kingdom* by Donald Kemp (1949) and *The Little Kingdom: A Record Chiefly of Central City in the Early Days* by Lynn Perrigo (1934).

Many of the local histories deal chiefly with personalities, and if that is your area of interest, you'll find fertile ground all through the old issues of *Colorado Magazine*, the journal of the state's historical society. Particularly interesting is Caroline Bancroft's July 1943 article: "The Elusive Figure of John H. Gregory, Discoverer of the First Gold Lode in Colorado." The *History of Clear Creek and Boulder Valleys* (1880) has a lot of obscure details and excellent engravings. There is also a three-book series published by the Central City Opera House (1932, 1934, and 1936) entitled *The Glory that was Gold*.

In the realm of personal observations and opinions are Samuel Bowles' 1869 book, *The Switzerland of America* and Frank Young's *Echoes from Arcadia* (1903). For a miner's recollections of the Argo Tunnel, find Merle Sowell's *Historical Highlights of Idaho Springs* (1976).

If you would like to go back to the original source on mining history, try the classic *The Mines of Colorado* by Ovando Hollister 1867 and republished in 1974 by Promontory Press). A little later was another excellent view by Frank Fossett in his *Colorado: Its Gold and Silver Mines, Farms and Stock Ranges, and Health and Pleasure Resorts* (1879, republished in 1975 by Rio Grande Press). John Canfield's *Mines and Mining Men of Colorado* (1893) is also good. If you're interested in a good history of the early discoveries around Denver, be sure to read Robert Brown's *The Great Pikes Peak Gold Rush* (1985).

For more general accounts that relate Colorado mining to developments elsewhere across the West, you should look up *Mining Frontiers of the Far West* by Rodman Paul (1963). In 1976, Otis Young published two superb explanations of how mining really was done in the West: *Western Mining* and *Black Powder and Hand Steel: Miners and Machines on the Old Western Frontier*. One of my all-time favorites is *The Miners*, a well-done book written in 1976 by Robert Wallace for the Time-Life series, "The Old West."

There are three collections of old photographs that I feel are the hands-down best: *Colorado Mining: A Photographic History* (1977) and *Secure the Shadow: Lachlan McLean, Colorado Mining Photographer* (1980), both by Duane Smith. Of course, don't forget to look at *Colorado on Glass* (1975) by Terry Mangan.

James Fell wrote one of the very few books on smelting, and he covers Nathaniel Hill and the Colorado smelting industry in depth. See *Ore to Metals: The Rocky Mountain Smelting Industry* (1979).

For more on the geology, I feel three United States Geological Survey works to be the best: *Economic Geology of Gilpin County and Adjacent Parts of Clear Creek and Boulder Counties* (Professional Paper 94, 1917, by Edson Bastin and James Hill), *Mining in Colorado* (Professional Paper 138 by Charles Henderson, 1926), and *Economic Geology of the Central City District* (Professional Paper 359 by Paul Sims, A.A. Drake, and E.W. Tooker, 1963).

Of more specialized interest is Mallory Ferrell's *The Gilpin Gold Tram: Colorado's Unique Narrow-Gauge* (1970). Weekend prospectors will find Ben Parker's two-volume "Gold Placers of Colorado" invaluable (originally published in the *Quarterly of the Colorado School of Mines*, vol. 69, #3, 1974 and now available for public sale).

The intent of this book has been to introduce people to some of the fascinating history hiding behind the old mine buildings and under the tailing piles around Central City. If you would like to delve into some of the subjects further, here are a few suggestions:

To learn more about the geology, try the libraries of the United States Geological Survey or the Colorado School of Mines; both are located in Golden. If you would like to see some of the gold and other minerals found around Central City and Black Hawk, go to the Museum of the School of Mines; their collection is extensive.

Historical research is really enjoyable, especially when you find yourself searching out details few others know about. You will find very competent and helpful people at all the libraries in the Denver area, but the most complete collections are at the Western History Department of the Denver Public Library and across the street at the Colorado Historical Society.

If you're interested in mine maps, the last two libraries are excellent places to try. The Colorado School of Mines library also has maps of a number of obscure mines, but the best collection overall is at the Bureau of Mines in the Denver Federal Center.

Old photos are like gold—they're where you find them. Most of the photographs used in this book came from the Denver Public Library, the Colorado Historical Society, and the Western History Department of the University of Colorado in Boulder.

# INDEX

All named mines, shafts, and veins are grouped together under the heading "Mines and Veins."

Quartz Hill Tunnel, 68, 85

Railroads
  Colorado Centra, 26, 76, 107, 109
  Colorado Southern, 34, 84–87, 107, 109
  Gilpin Railroad, 34, 109, 114
  Gilpin Tramway, 34, 35, 69, 70, 109, 114

Ralston, Louis, 3

Ralston Creek, 3, 5

Raymond, Rossiter, 20, 21, 25, 28

Rees, R.T., 11

Russell Gulch, 9, 16, 34, 82, 87

Russell Gulch district, 12

Russell, William Greene, 3, 4, 8

Sleepy Hollow Mine disaster, 37, 74, 109

sluice, 12, 111

smelting, general, 17, 20, 24–29, 107

smelting companies: *See* American Smelting and Refining Company, Boston & Colorado Smelting Company, and Denver Smelting Company

South Platte River, 3, 4

Standley, Joseph, 67

sulfides, 14–17

Swansea, Wales, 24, 25, 26

Tunnel, Argo 36, 37–40, 44, 46, 56, 68, 80, 82, 88, 89, 109, 113
  Bobtail, 43, 56, 61, 62, 72
  LaCrosse, 56, 65, 85, 86
  Newhouse, *See* Argo Tunnel
  Quartz Hill, 68, 85

uranium, 44, 45, 109

Vasquez Fork *See* Clear Creek

veins, general, 49–51, 111, map 52